AF820994

Basic Entrepreneurship

Raushan Gross, PhD

Basic Entrepreneurship

ISBN: 978-1-948915-18-2

NORTH
AMERICAN BUSINESS
PRESS

North American Business Press
Atlanta, Georgia
Miami, Florida
New York, New York,
Toronto, Canada

First Printing, 2021

Acknowledgements

After authoring many other types of written works, I now have a far greater appreciation for anyone who has travelled down the path of writing a book.

To my wife and kids, who allowed me to write this book, who seemed interested in what I wrote about in this book, who allowed me space at the dinner table to compose it, and who listened to me talk about its contents—thank you.

To my mother, who kept me focused on the fact that this is my first book and not the last—thank you.

Larry, thank you for introducing me to many great writings and philosophies ranging from economics and history that have found their place in this book.

To Mrs. Dee, who gave me continuous encouragement over the years that helped shape the creation of this work—thank you.

Rose, thank you for adding value at every phase of this work that helped it all come together.

And thank you, Pfeiffer University, for the support of intellectual endeavors such as this.

The Kitchen Table

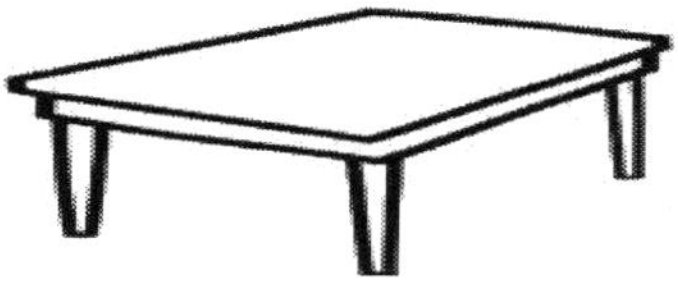

Table of Contents

Introduction

"Persons of genius, it is true, are, and are always likely to be, a small minority; but in order to have them, it is necessary to preserve the soil in which they grow."

John S. Mill, 1859[1]

Since the beginning of time, society has acknowledged people who make a living creating goods and providing services to those residing nearby and far away. These people—whom we call entrepreneurs—have garnered certain acclaim and hold a pivotal role in the market economy. People who decide to provide a product or service that helps other people meet needs or reach goals express the enterprising spirit that differentiates them from other market participants. While collaborating with other individuals and society at large, entrepreneurs act individually but spontaneously in a way that some might see as irregular. These entrepreneurial people or groups (in a cultural or regional sense of the term, or a collection of common practices) were the suppliers and traders of necessary goods and services to the general population that surrounded them. What is noticeable about these people or groups of people is their societal standing—known, throughout the ages, as people who existed on society's fringe. Historically speaking, prior to the Industrial Revolution, entrepreneurial individuals associated with cultural groups that were not part of the aristocracy were looked down upon and found it difficult to compete with those in the landed aristocracy involved in trade. Certainly, the groups on the fringes found methods to trade. Times have changed; now, the entrepreneur is known as the creator, innovator, and purveyor of market knowledge.

Most of society views entrepreneurs as unique in their thinking and action—as individuals who do not succumb to the status quo. These people do not offer to the masses the usual and typical but the rare

[1] Mill, J.S. (1998) On Liberty. New York: NY: Oxford world's Classics

and unique—items and wares they think will become necessary to others' way of life. They go to the market; the market does not go to them. Entrepreneurs' objective is to provide a good that is better than what others offer. In some cases, entrepreneurs collaborate with a producer and work as a middleman to sell to the consumer.[2] Serving customers in remote places thousands of miles from their homes was not unfamiliar to early entrepreneurs—nor to today's.

There have always been individuals or groups of culturally connected peoples across various regions who did not consider themselves entrepreneurs as we commonly use the term today. The producer-entrepreneur and the capitalist-entrepreneur finds its origin with the early Irish-French economist and writer Richard Cantillon.[3] In some ways the term entrepreneur contains a similar connotation as it did in the days of Cantillon, but in many regards this notion has changed. Today's entrepreneur deals in more industries than agriculture and encounters many regulations and complex social relationships than the 18th century conception of the use of resources to bring to market for consumer consumption. Economists, namely those of the Austrian School, have ascribed great power to the entrepreneur, often referring to their role power as the driving force behind the market process.[4]

For centuries, every aspect of an entrepreneur has been studied, including personality, decision-making ability, capital accumulation, mindset, environment in which they originate, immigration and emigration, culture, institutions, and their methods of eliminating high production costs. The research on entrepreneurship is extensive. Many veins have been investigated: the operation of small businesses, capitalists and capitalism, entrepreneurial firms, and the customer orientation of entrepreneurship. There has been other offshoots, such as regional economics and the transmission of human capital and knowledge

---

[2] Light, I., & Gold, S. (2000). *Ethnic economies*. San Diego, CA: Academic Press.
[3] Cantillon, R. (2010). *An essay on economic theory*. Alabama, AL: Ludwig von Mises Institute.
[4] Huerta de Soto, J. (2008). *The Austrian School: Market order and entrepreneurial creativity*. Northampton, MA: Edward Elgar.

between entrepreneurial networks. This book dives into the main arteries of entrepreneurship to weave a foundational view into a contemporary understanding of this growing and essential topic. It also explores the historical context of economic and entrepreneurial thinkers.

Entrepreneurship is, and always has been, an anomalous market activity that involves not just a good idea or two but a vision that emanates from the individual—an individual vision that is supplemented with the requisite skills, human capital, and environment. These factors must come together and be applied to an entrepreneurial opportunity for an entrepreneurial vision to materialize. A common misconception is that only certain people can become entrepreneurs. This view is false. Who becomes an entrepreneur is largely determined by the time and market conditions being ripe for an individual's entrepreneurial plans to come to fruition. One example is Booker T. Washington,[5] who saw himself the new president of a university—which in his mind was built and ready to admit students. However, when he reached his destination, he found instead nothing but empty land, upon which later arose Tuskegee University. Washington acted upon his vision for a university through the use of skills, capital, and determination. As Washington famously stated, "drop your bucket where you are."

The entrepreneur is not the sole arbiter of the market. Surprisingly, little has to do with the entrepreneurs' characteristics per se. What matters most to entrepreneurial success is market demand, market knowledge, production factors, and market participants. Even Richard Cantillon said that personality plays an insignificant role and is of no consequence to the entrepreneur's formation: "even beggars and robbers are....entrepreneurs."[6] The market is a social phenomenon, and the one personal attribute an entrepreneur needs is foresight.[7]The entrepreneur is one factor of

---

[5] Washington, T. B. (1986). Booker t. Washington: Up From Slavery. New York, NY: Penguin Classics.

[6] Ibid., p. 13.

[7] Hebert, F. R., & Link, N. A. (1982). *The entrepreneur*. New York, NY: Praeger.

production, and is dependent on other factors that must come together.

For instance, Alexander Graham Bell developed elocution techniques, which led him to develop the telephone—not surprising. He and his family were students of elocution, the phonautograph, and multiple telegraph. His grandfather investigated treatments for the hearing impaired. At an early age, Bell was introduced to leading members of the Philological Society, particularly Sir Charles Wheatstone, and lived in London when the idea of sound and sound transmission was a hotbed of innovation and discussion.[8] Bell's mother's unfortunate loss of hearing in his early life propelled his ideas in the field of elocution. In this instance, it is clear that things came together from many aspects of life to prepare Alexander Graham Bell and his new invention for the marketplace.

Unsurprisingly, knowledge and production factors may not come together in a specific time or place to allow an entrepreneurial vision to materialize for some people, but that is for another book. Theorist in the area of entrepreneurship has left the role of timing out of the entrepreneurial discussion, as the passing of time is vital to understand what customers demand or a need that has yet to reveal itself in the market. *Consumers* are the drivers of entrepreneurial production and market activity. The question is whether the entrepreneur can bring to market economic goods that are useful to the aims of others whom they do not know. Where there is perceived opportunity in a marketplace, the entrepreneurs tend to use their personal factors of production in pursuit of the perceived opportunity. Knowledge is transmitted to individual entrepreneurs via a number of social institutions and the economic system, which provides signals to entrepreneurs. Entrepreneurs use these signals as new knowledge to make forecast on uncertain opportunities and market discoveries. The entrepreneur subjectively understands market situations better than anyone else, and they become aware of the conditions of a market economy due to differences that are

---

[8] Costain, T. B. (1960). *The chord of steel: The story of the invention of the telephone*. New York, NY: Doubleday & Co.

inherent in product or service quality, price or locations that could be better conveyed to the future consumer. That is, two people can conceivably look at the same thing and understand it differently; therefore, just the sheer subjective opportunity costs of one person can align with demand behavior to justify the imperative to grasp the market opportunity.

Oddly enough, if one were to say the word *entrepreneur* in conversation, the listener might assume something vastly different than what the speaker meant, and vice versa. There is a tendency to use the term entrepreneur in various contexts where that word presumably once had a narrower meaning than it does now. Today, the entrepreneur works within an extremely complex market and numerous industries and relies on an intricate web of supply networks.

In some cases, entrepreneurs decide to make venturing start-ups a lifestyle, conducting business on a full-time basis. Others, however, are displaced or terminated from full-time employment and turn to self-ownership opportunities. It is relatively easy to become an entrepreneur, either passively or as a lifestyle, by using one's capital and resources. Examples include providing business-to-business services in photography or website architecture, or any other number of enterprises. Being part of a family business is another consideration for some who want to leave a legacy.

As opposed to the conventional entrepreneur, there is the corporate entrepreneur—those working under a corporation's auspices and charged with spotting opportunity using corporate resources. Although the concept of corporate entrepreneurship is not well-defined, the premise rest of the foundations of the Schumpeterian notion of the individual novelty in the use of resources that changes the pattern of existing resources and processes, namely the pattern of equilibrium and competition. Corporate entrepreneurs seek innovative ways to combine and recombine resources to develop new to market ideas. The corporate entrepreneur goes against the convention that there is perfect knowledge and competitive advantages in a given industry. Other than Joseph Schumpeter, Henry Mintzberg said that entrepreneurial firms are aggressive and seek out risky new markets and maneuver within bureaucratic constraints.[9] Perhaps the only difference between the corporate version of entrepreneurship and, say, an author, is the personal realization of profits and losses. Some use the term *corporate entrepreneurship* in a corporate sense—where managers act entrepreneurially to gain market share by responding to consumer demands using innovative methods within a corporate structure. If individuals think outside of the box or enlarge the box, they are generally acting entrepreneurially within and outside a firm. The realization of profits and losses is the line of demarcation between those who reap market opportunity and shoulder the burden of risks, and those who do not.

An environment where entrepreneurship can flourish is one where all of the entrepreneurial elements can come together. That includes the right space and time, productive skills, positive attitudes toward market endeavors in general, and capital in particular. Finding opportunities to provide a good or service important to a market participant is but half the battle. There is also a need to have a market where buyer and seller—customer and entrepreneur—can exchange economic goods of lesser value. Economic systems and environments matter greatly. Some sectors of the economy will always need entrepreneurs to offer a service or produce a product that consumers demand. Until there are machines that can provide services without human intervention (think of barbers and hairstylists), there will be an environment conducive to entrepreneurs' prosperity.

Continuing the same line of thought, let us assume barbers and hair stylists' own supplies and incur either a profit or loss as a result of providing services to customers. Both the barber and stylist must own tools to provide a service. Without ownership of tools of production to provide a service, they would not be able to ascertain the effects of either profits or losses. Therefore, ownership of the tools of production is a vital aspect to the success or failure of the

---

[9] Mintzberg, H. (1989). *Mintzberg on management: Inside our strange world of organizations*. New York, NY: Simon and Schuster.

barber or hair stylist. This example to be extended in any entrepreneurial factor of production, where the use of the factor of production has to be assessed as it is used for consumer purposes. Therefore, the economic system that allow entrepreneurs to own factors of production provides a basic calculation to determine whether or not the endeavor is worth the entrepreneur time and use of resources.

Market dynamics demanding resource awareness and profit and loss are common connections that make one wonder about the best environment for entrepreneurship to thrive. While there are conditions that can aid or hamper entrepreneurship, there lacks a basic approach of how entrepreneurship works. Economic systems of all types exist across the globe, yet there is a fair bit of entrepreneurial activity throughout those economic systems. Regional and cultural drivers add to the propensity for a greater or less amount of entrepreneurship across each economic system. Specific economic systems and cultural drivers determine the robustness of the role entrepreneurs play within those very systems. Again, entrepreneurship requires a favorable environment and favorable institutions where all the skills and strengths of resources of the entrepreneur can come together and be put to good use and to allow for individual expression.

If we think about what entrepreneurship is, we might say that waking up in the morning is entrepreneurial. Why? Well, because you decided to move from one state to the next without knowing the events that might unfold the moment you step out of bed. Just getting out of bed is a sign that you are eager to grasp whatever opportunity you may encounter that day.

Observing, and acting on those observations, is the essential mindset of the entrepreneur. Noticing and understanding the potential of an opportunity speaks to the very nature of the entrepreneur. What is it that entrepreneurially minded people notice that others do not? Often, they notice what others miss or may not care about. Entrepreneurs can sense opportunities that others do not sense, care about, or notice. Do you take the time to understand the mechanics of how your coffee machine works, or do you just put your coffee pod in the machine and tap the start button?

How might we define or categorize these keen observations of opportunity? There are many specific attributes, characteristics, and definitions related to the function and type of entrepreneur. Robert Hebert and Albert Link provided a list of the function and type of entrepreneurs:[10]

- The entrepreneur is the person who assumes the risk associated with uncertainty.
- The entrepreneur is the person who supplies financial capital.
- The entrepreneur is an innovator.
- The entrepreneur is a decision-maker.
- The entrepreneur is an industrial leader.
- The entrepreneur is a manager or superintendent.
- The entrepreneur is an organizer and coordinator of economic resources.
- The entrepreneur is the owner of an enterprise.
- The entrepreneur is a contractor.
- The entrepreneur is an arbitrageur.
- The entrepreneur is an allocator of resources among alternative uses.

Indeed, an individual who assumes any of these characteristics outlined by Hebert and Link can observe customers' future needs and anticipate the best use of the entrepreneur's production factors. There are a number of ways entrepreneurs are able to sense the unseen—to understand their customers' satisfaction and dissatisfaction and respond to the demands. Nothing exciting—just observation. Just the mundane stuff that everyone else overlooks.

This book steers away from a complex conceptualization of entrepreneurship. The proceeding chapters convey the social need for the entrepreneur, but more importantly, how the entrepreneur respond to the complex, spurious, and unpredictable nature of

---

[10] Hebert, R. F., & Link, A. (2010, June 21). Historical perspectives on the entrepreneur. *Foundations and Trends in Entrepreneurship*, *2*(4).

market phenomenon that lay outside of the aspects of their aimed at endeavors. Entrepreneurship can be described not to deter those aspiring to be entrepreneurs and those who seek entrepreneurship. In short, entrepreneurs seek to use up capital and resource in an effort to challenge risks. Entrepreneurs grasp at the opportunity to bring products and services to the market, and, in many regards, carry out this market function as a lifestyle.

This book explains what entrepreneurship is in its most basic form, as well as its variations and competing market complexities. This book provides a basic idea of entrepreneurship for those who want not a *how to* understanding of the topic, but a *what is* understanding, and perhaps a fresh approach to entrepreneurial basics. To a degree, this book lays out a reality that has, over time, become romanticized. The entrepreneur, no matter their IQ or the unique offerings they hold dear, function at the whims of consumers and the market process—this is a foundational aspect of entrepreneurial understanding.

Surprisingly, the *basic* understanding of entrepreneurship is not well explained in today's general literature. This void poses an opportunity for this text to provide a full, basic understanding of the essential role it plays in a market economy. The text covers the main arteries about the subjectivity of entrepreneurship and, along the way, covers the main crosscurrents in which it intersects with culture, attitude, human capital, competition and markets, value, and production.

This book is for the student, nascent entrepreneur, and those interested in entrepreneurship's basic foundational ideas. The approach tends toward those who believe that the fewer barriers to market entry, the better, and that entrepreneurs and society are interdependent, while they are dependent on each other to bring to market products and services that ease each other's dissatisfaction. The reader must understand the non-technical, entrepreneurial spirit of entrepreneurship, which is often the deciding factor of success in the long run when the naysayers assume that an entrepreneurial endeavor is showing signs of failure.

The fundamental aspects of entrepreneurship are vital in understanding the role of profit and loss. Entrepreneurs' vision, steadfastness, and resilience have somehow beat out technical naysayers throughout history. Most successful businesses started as a result of someone's vision to help others, whether it be with cosmetics, vehicles, tools, or replaceable parts for machinery—in most cases, the odds were stacked against them and they were told their idea would never work. But it did!

I choose not to cover the technical how-to's in this book. Instead, I intend to speak of entrepreneurship in terms of its most fundamental level—the entrepreneur's role as the center of market activity within institutional frameworks. It has been my observation that capital is not needed to become or remain an entrepreneur. Someone with capital who believes in a new venture will support a promising star. What *is* needed is a sense of timing and discovery and an understanding of the nature of entrepreneurship.

This book focuses on more basic entrepreneurial insights in plain language and prose. I do not seek to project what people should do but to explain the primary and most fundamental underpinnings of an extremely complex role of engaging in entrepreneurship in a market economy. It is plain to you as it is to me—the entrepreneur needs a market, and markets need entrepreneurs. Moreover, customers need entrepreneurs, and entrepreneurs need customers.

Chapter 1: Entrepreneurs are Different

"[Johann Sebastian] Bach was not so much a revolutionary as an improver, reformer, and systematic innovator. He did not abandon any form, but changed and rarefied it." [11]

Paul Johnson, 2006

Many people think and talk about competition with a little uneasiness because of the connotations it carries. Competition, in the positive sense of the term, can be a non-rivalrous action that can bring about great results. Two or three competitors can work toward the same end—customers—and be rewarded. There is always room for healthy competition. Generally, only the entrepreneur—most often the newcomer—feels comfort about competition in the marketplace. Most people do not understand the entrepreneur's sense of competitiveness. The common saying goes, "If it ain't broke, don't fix it"—but it's not so for the entrepreneur! Innovation does not happen in a vacuum, and ideas can only be implemented in the context of the ideas that came before.

Most people like the idea of comfort and predictability—don't rock the boat! But there are times when change and something new are warranted—whether it is making decisions in the marketplace, changing the allocation of resources to better suit consumers' value, making better use of resources for products that are cost-prohibitive, or trying to make a product that's better than those already on the market. Many people accept that change will happen at some point; most would agree that the direction it will take boils down to the means and not the ends.

Why and how do entrepreneurial people create discomfort in others? Is the discomfort that entrepreneurs create good or bad for those who are not entrepreneurial? The entrepreneur sees the market differently than the non-entrepreneur. Ludwig von Mises, Israel

---

[11] Johnson, P. (2007) Creators From Chaucer To Walt Disney. London, UK: Phoenix.

Kirzner, Murray Rothbard, and Robert Hebert all identified a full range of the characteristics and attributes of entrepreneurs. Entrepreneurs are dissenters from the status quo. They not only use products or services, but feel compelled to provide them in a way that is better and less expensive. Why shouldn't they? In contrast, non-entrepreneurs are effectively the end-users of products in the marketplace.

Entrepreneurs use their aquired skills to unlock potential in things that others overlook. Some say that entrepreneurs are individuals who tend to discover novel products for the mundane uses of customers. Entrepreneurs have historically looked for something new when faced with dissatisfaction. This market action makes non-entrepreneurial types uncomfortable because it necessitates competition. Entrepreneurs think about problems (related to products and or services) systemically and think about how products can be problematic when they want to make a purchase. This type of thinking is not surprising, since entrepreneurs are characteristically discoverers and promoters and apply their tacit and knowledge-based judgment at a particular point in time. As business owners strive to increase market share, this leads competitors to the unpleasant task of coming up with new, creative, and innovative business ideas to continue to compete. An extremely entrepreneurial person will continuously find new ways of playing tug of war with other industry competitors.

Who really enjoys competition? Who enjoys competition when all of one's assets and capital are on the line? Not all entrepreneurs are competitive to the same degree, and not all entrepreneurs are open to changes in customer preferences as a result of new knowledge which creates new conditions that alters ones decision-making data on product prices and resource availability. For many business owners, hearing of a new upstart (or start-up) in the same industry can turn a smile into a frown. Competition tends to not be congenial. But entrepreneurial competitive behaviors start with ideas and creativity that plays out in the marketplace.

In the market, or in a firm, entrepreneurial action provides the fuel for the constant mining of consumer value. If entrepreneurs cease acting this way, customers will cease to see innovation and growing value in the marketplace. The tension between new ideas and predictability makes entrepreneurs vital to our economy. More than anything else, entrepreneurs explore ideas that make others uncomfortable. When ideas clash, it creates friction among entrepreneurs, all vying for similar results—seeking to acquire definite ends with dissimilar means. Such clashes cause competition in the market, which some might view as insidious. But on the contrary, competition is a necessary teacher for entrepreneurs.

You know that you are in the company of an entrepreneur when that person articulates out-of-the-box ideas. Ideas tend to make the box bigger for others. Non-entrepreneurial people may overlook the thinking and creativity of entrepreneurs, but they feel the sting of discomfort. Instead of protecting a turf, non-entrepreneurs should embrace the fact that competition is an inevitable part of market activity—it is the ultimate form of cooperation.

There is a sharp contrast between entrepreneurs and those who are not. First, it is the entrepreneurial nature to do things that others may have thought absurd, ridiculous, or "would never work." Entrepreneurs remain steadfast in acquiring knowledge both a priori and a posteriori to make profits and deliver value to customers. Second, entrepreneurs are not afraid to challenge uncertainty. Possessing both subjective knowledge about a given market and a nimble spirit, entrepreneurs do not stick to predictability, but understand the likelihood that yesterday is past, and that tomorrow's preferences, tastes, and styles will differ. This kind of thinking and attitude makes competitors uncomfortable, which changes the business landscape's level of competitive behavior.

Market competition should increase congenial rivalry and not elicit discomfort, even within a firm, where internal entrepreneurs vie to implement ideas. Competition is healthy for all involved. However, this assumption may be far from true in practice. The reality is that people with entrepreneurial characteristics are seen as outsiders or dissenters, even if their intentions are not to act as such. Those who feel uncomfortable about competition may fall in the range of business owners, managers, and/or industry competitors.

Even family members might not appreciate the entrepreneur in the family who wants to rearrange furniture to make more—or better use—of space. People without entrepreneurial characteristics might find entrepreneurs challenging to understand or comprehend because of their vast knowledge and attitude toward the most novel ideas that seem impracticable to most.

The entrepreneur is qualitatively different from other market participants. First, entrepreneurs assume a great deal of risk, though their risk in operating a venture earns them special rewards. Entrepreneurs are not more intelligent than others, despite what some may contend. Instead, they reap the benefits of circumstances of time, place, and experience. When these factors come together, it is the individual entrepreneur who moves first in a direction in which circumstances present opportunities.

Moreover, some entrepreneurs (e.g., Steve Jobs, Daymond John, Mary Kay, and the New England Peddler—among a whole host of others who are nameless) seek to mold their circumstances. Some, who do not have fame behind their name, have similar stories. Creating and being aware of favorable circumstances is what makes the entrepreneur quite different from other market participants.

John Stewart Mills discussed important aspect of the social development of individuality in his famous work, *On Liberty*, which presents the social role of individuality that aligns with the characterization of the entrepreneur's vision, independence, and life experiences causing them to pursue their market discoveries that serve others' needs within a social system.[12] Mills provided a list of factors related to individuality, such as having individual thoughts and feelings, pursuing tasks while possessing freedom of conscience, and accumulating life experiences. Why then is the entrepreneur self-interested? Actually, they are not self-interested, they are however, view opportunity objectively. Although entrepreneurs embrace their individuality, they have a keen sense of collaboration. Their heightened sense of individuality leads them to believe in and pursue their vision despite what others believe.

[12] Mill, J.S. (1998) On Liberty. New York: NY: Oxford world's Classics

Individuals have a vision for themselves, even in the social context of their family, and their community. Entrepreneurs collaborate with others within a community, family, or within a country or across many countries to reach a market for their vision. While they collaborate with their network, they maintain their individuality.

Entrepreneurs also have a knack for seeing the big picture and seeing themselves as the primary casting character within it. Entrepreneurs cast their visions for others to attach to and collaborate. The entrepreneur initially has the vision; others follow. The big picture is not so much what they can sell to buyers—that is a relatively small detail—the big picture is the markets conditions and whether or not they are favorable or unfavorable. Secondary, are how resources are flowing from one industry to the next to their most urgent needs, and how customers preferences change over time. They have vision and see opportunities. Non-entrepreneurially minded people may have just as much awareness of what the market is doing but little interest in pursuing their vision in this way.

How entrepreneurs act makes them different because they understand that something is waiting to be discovered by them, and that time is of the essence. The saying goes, "time is money." This saying reflects the mindset of the entrepreneur, which makes them different from others who do not consider time with the same urgency. The market and its changes have a way of influencing the entrepreneur's time horizon. They are aware of and consider market shifts, asking themselves, is it a time of prosperity, recession, or recovery?

Chapter 2: Basic Entrepreneurship

"This is the constitutional limitation of man's knowledge and interests, the fact that he cannot know more than a tiny part of the whole of society and that therefore all that can enter into his motives are the immediate effects which his actions will have in the sphere he knows."

Friedrich A. von Hayek, 1948

The term entrepreneur implies that there are economic activities this person can do to serve others. There is a tendency for one to think that entrepreneurs are productive only for themselves. From the start, there is an idea and vision one has about their particular situation and/or their circumstances in which they envision product or service enhancements. The entrepreneurial function seems vague, but vague is how things look to many entrepreneurs until they discover a market opportunity. Entrepreneurs consider the vast number of potential buyers and sellers who may partake of or abstain from their entrepreneurial vision in the form of a profit or loss. While entrepreneurs are individuals, their vision creates a harmonious link between market participants. Thus, we say that entrepreneurs act based on changes in customer preferences. The "entrepreneur is acting in regard to the changes occurring in the data of the market."[13]

It is not the who the entrepreneur is, per se, that is the important question—the more important question is the function they play in a market economy. Whether known or unknown, seen or unseen, the entrepreneurial function is irreplaceable in what they do for consumers and producers in terms of resource shifts, prices, and economic prosperity. Ultimately, the question of who an entrepreneur *is* fails to consider the market forces that constrain what they can and cannot do in a market economy. For the most part,

---

[13] von Mises, L. (1988). *Human action: A treatise on economics*. Auburn, AL: Ludwig von Mises Institute.

customers only see the visual artifacts of entrepreneurs' human energy and the final good derived from their vision and the application of knowledge accumulated over time. Their unseen vision and accumulated knowledge are an unobservable fact.

Knowledge is acquired over time from previous work experience, education (both formal and informal), family, and other social and cultural surroundings. When the market opportunity arises, the entrepreneur sees something that others do not. This vision, we can assume, arises from accumulated experiences, leading them the entrepreneur to use different means to reach an end inspired by customer dissatisfaction. We can assume this is the difference between seeing and acting—the difference between knowing what entrepreneurship is and how entrepreneurship works.

Entrepreneurs, and those of that ilk, have historically been agile visionaries, discoverers, promotors, inventors, innovators, capitalists, and even customers. Albert Einstein's theory of relativity and Vincent van Gogh's *Starry Night* both resulted from an entrepreneurial pursuit. In their day and today, these are unexpected artifacts of knowledge, discovery, and innovative thinking that went beyond the status quo to enrich the lives of others in both educational and aesthetic ways. In their time, these works were not viewed in the same way as they are today—then and now, we might agree that Einstein and van Gogh were both market disrupters.

The term disruption connotes a negative conflict between what people have done or process put in place as a standard and then a new process that is more effective comes along that sweeps it away. Joseph Schumpeter talked about innovative disruption quite a bit, and many authors have agreed with his foundational thought on the entrepreneur. In his view, we can consider the act of disruption as enhancing something that exists but adding a unique twist. Einstein did this with relativity; he added to existing mathematical concepts from a new angle that led to a breakthrough.

Looking at this another way, customers are agile, innovative discoverers in the market. The customer as entrepreneur is not discussed often—or not at all—in the mainstream literature. But customers seek to gain the best exchange with a seller or business, one that works within their subjective valuation. Customers are innovative, try new products, and use them in ways unintended by the entrepreneur-producer. In many instances, customers or users of products find new and unintended uses for items, most of which were outside of the entrepreneur-producer's scope.

In theory, everyone is an entrepreneur. But we cannot take this notion too far because entrepreneurial action always aims at making one's situation better than it was before acting. Some people may act but not in the sense of acting for betterment. With that, when people act they either incur losses by acting in error or profit by making the correct decision. Acting implies a risk and uncertainty that cannot be foreseen. Customers incur risk when deciding on a seller to purchase products or services from; although, this is less of a risk than the producer-entrepreneur. More often than not, an individual is willing to be the customer-entrepreneur and not the producer-entrepreneur because the customer-entrepreneur does not encounter or is not subject to the unforeseen risks inherent in pursuing market-based opportunities. Only the entrepreneur sees the need for adjustment through the clutter and takes the initiative to pursue it, regardless of the odds they face.

One entrepreneurial condition that is commonly overlooked is market error. Error in judgment, investment, and action is a reality in the sense that if not viewed and examined as to what causes the error, both consumers and entrepreneurs continuously fall into the same state of losses. The same continuous errors in market investments and pursuits and seeing the wrong opportunities create static results. Nothing about the world or the market is static. Even if we tried to make it so, people would need and seek out food, shelter, and community, among other bare necessities that require individuals of all walks of life (i.e., producers, sellers, customers, firms, suppliers, and retailers) to cooperate and produce higher-level goods for later consumption.

The entrepreneur is not omniscient and is prone to make mistakes and errors in judgment about market opportunities. My assertion is a breakaway from the often-omniscient caricature of the entrepreneur, which is in much of the narrative of the *successful entrepreneur*. There is no such thing as a standard approach to market entry because entrepreneurs are always at the whims of change and tumult. Therefore, we have to look at things as they are in light of what entrepreneurs are subjected to in the real world.

The real-world application of entrepreneurship does not view mistakes, poor investments, and other human infallibilities as unfavorable. It is simply reality that people are not omnipotent or omniscient. Entrepreneurs and customers are participants in a market process that involves a constant shift between changes and adaptations to tastes and the rising or falling of product/service importance on customers value scales. Geniuses create from their ideas and consumers' reactions to their ideas and creations are always up for judgment and critique. People say that businesses tend to fail in their first few years of operation as if this is a natural phenomenon. The reality is that market participants vote and decide what is brought to them to the market. Entrepreneurs are either voted in or out of the market by customers who are users of the final goods produced or services offered, and then seek other employment. Why? Because capital is scarce, time is scarce, and energy is scarce, which is why people who were entrepreneurs find other, more rewarding paths to blaze that do not interlock risks with their assets. They are called displaced entrepreneurs. Perhaps scarcity goes beyond this cursory explanation, given that mistakes and errors are due to knowledge or lack thereof, for no one person has full knowledge about anything. The world is too dynamic for one person to possess all there is to know or understand. Entrepreneurs, in effect ,are purveyors of knowledge to people whom they do not know. For instance, knowledge as a corrector of error is a function of exchange between customer and entrepreneur that signals to both who will serve them best, which plays a vital part to competition thus creating facts creating new circumstantial learning for the entrepreneur.

The production of any product is risky. In the real world, an entrepreneur-seller of many goods may find that what was once was in vogue is no longer popular. There is no certainty in customer choice or preference as time passes. Another consideration is that the price of money and labor influences plans and production opportunities. A profit opportunity that was once a viable option for an entrepreneur may no longer be so due to changes in their country's fiscal, monetary, and or regulatory policies. Equipment for future use may not work as intended, and credit to procure equipment is subject to the cost of production, the price of money, and the amount of money in circulation. These financial matters are essential for anyone who seeks to produce a final customer good or service that requires raw materials. There are of course market constraints that can hamper the functions of the entrepreneur and the grasping of the potential market opportunities.

Of particular notice are the roles of purveyors and conveyors in the market economy. The next time you purchase a coffee or tea, a painting, dental work, or an electronic gadget, consider the many factors had to come together, despite the barriers to trade and regulations raised against the entrepreneur both before and after the good was brought to market. The basic: entrepreneurs need markets, and markets need entrepreneurs. Entrepreneurs and markets need ingenuity, naivety, and people willing to pursue new products for new markets and new products for old markets.[14] By its very nature, entrepreneurship requires the use of competitive advantages to ensure others will not serve customers better than you. Advantages can come in many forms, and they cannot last forever. The entrepreneur's role is to attempt to take what exists and try to produce it better at a lower cost or better quality.

Understanding the influence of the market cycle is imperative. In a fast-cycle market, it is relatively inexpensive to imitate a product or service. In a fast-cycle market, imitators are rampant. A standard-cycle market can somewhat protect entrepreneurial offerings from imitators. A slow-cycle market differs from the others; in one, it is costly for imitators who attempt to replicate the entrepreneurial business products and services. Imitation is inherent in most business activities involving profits made using similarly held resources, called the factors of production. The production

---

[14] Boorstin, D. J. (1965). *The Americans: The national experience.* New York, NY: Random House.

factors: entrepreneurship, land, labor, capital is needed to produce a good or service for customers. All production factors are needed, especially the factor this book describes—entrepreneurship. These production factors come together to meet customers' most urgent and essential needs.

What protects the entrepreneur? Customer choice. This may seem paradoxical, but the more choices a customer has, the more protection is provided to entrepreneurs in a market economy. The lack of customer choice is a sure bet that there is an equal loss to the entrepreneurial ranks. When customers cease to act—that is, stop seeking to make their current situation better and more profitable than their previous one—there is no need for the entrepreneur. Efficiently meeting customer demands has mostly been the result of entrepreneurs seeking to make their own lives better. Serving others to serve oneself can be traced back through history. When unfettered, the market has a built-in mechanism for creating an environment in which customers may choose to buy from those who offer the best quality and price—*this* is customer choice, and it is the bedrock of a market economy. This is the opposite of artificially created barriers that discourage potential entrepreneurs from entry. Barring potential start-ups from participating in customer choice poses problems for both entrepreneurship and customer choice. Customer choice does not detract from market opportunities; it strengthens the market for both entrepreneurs and customers.

Entrepreneurs naturally tend to cluster near one another. A few examples of entrepreneurial clustering are enclaves, ethnic regions, online affiliations—any grouping where buyers can easily choose from a host of sellers. A natural cluster of entrepreneurs brings about healthy competition, harmony, and cooperation. Again, competition is not intended to harm entrepreneurs but rather to be a teacher that makes everyone better—not the insidious type of competition, but the type we need to feed the spirit, intellect, and well-being. Open competition between entrepreneurs brings about customer choice—unlike deliberately formed ecosystems, which create artificially high entry barriers and disallow newcomer entrepreneurs from entering the market. Spontaneous ecosystems are like beehives to bumblebees because entrepreneurs can subjectively analyze their opportunity costs relative to their propensity to bring the discovery to fruition under a favorable market condition. .

Who is the entrepreneur? Many authors describe the entrepreneur from numerous perspectives often related to their market actions. The entrepreneur has unique insights into the needs of others. Often it is their characteristics that continue to be the talking points that explain their unique behavior (i.e., intelligence, passion, resilient, rugged, and ability to be a self-starter). However, there is also a more critical question: how does the entrepreneur function in the process of harmonious cooperation during economic phenomenon? In short, the entrepreneur is the initiator of market participants' demands. They are demand responders who use their factors of production to provide either a good or service to consumers in the most efficient manner. This makes it sound like the entrepreneur is beloved by everyone, as indeed, taking the risks inherent in the use of their resources in an attempt to better our lives seem like a tremendous task for an individual. Aside from the fact that entrepreneurs must also reinvest their resources in order to produce for further consumer consumption and their most urgent needs will change their preferences and perceptions, which explicitly changes the entrepreneurs use of their resources.

Conventional wisdom and entrepreneurship have a unique relationship. The economy's entrepreneurial function relies on conventional wisdom as a blueprint, but surely in the long-run there is no doubt emerging institutions that purvey entrepreneurial ideas and processes which can benefit society largely through innovative processes that are not to be discarded.[15] Conventional wisdom may lead one to believe that entrepreneurs are purely self-interested, in the sense that they do not collaborate with and are interested in others. However, the entrepreneur acts in a manner which is completely opposite this long-standing and misguided view rooted in convention.

---

[15] Klein, M. (2006). The Golden Age of the American Entrepreneur. Hillsdale, MI: Hillsdale College Press.

Take, for instance, a painter hired to create a few pieces on canvas for a client. Is it possible for the painter to complete the pieces without the collaboration of the buyer or company that will be their buyer? The artist and purchaser are part of a team once the contract is agreed upon—and more—the painter must find suppliers to procure the tools needed to complete the product (paintings) for the customer. Some view the entrepreneur, under the market system, is an "exploiter."[16] Since this is of course inaccurate, the entrepreneur should be seen as a servant who seeks the well-being of themselves and of their consumers. They are demand responders, serving customers. Entrepreneurs bringing products and services to customers, the market system functions to signal to the entrepreneur what is or is not wanted. For example, when hired, the painter then produces paintings that will either get rejected or accepted by potential or existing customers. The beauty of the market process and the entrepreneur's function is that success is measured, and failures are too. Success being the incentive that signals to others to follow suit.[17] Does it matter what type of personality the entrepreneur has or the market conditions in which can or cannot operate? Entrepreneurs living in two different regions of the world can possess the same skillsets or mindsets. They might even have the same or similar life experiences, let us say. But what is critical is not so much who the entrepreneur is; instead, it is the economy's entrepreneurial function. If we examine the function of the entrepreneur in one country is and what it is in another country, the answer reflects the degree to which one entrepreneur may have an environment that allows them to function at a higher level and be more productive than in another, where the entrepreneur encounters a whole separate set of institutions affecting their productivity and preventing a timely response to demanders.

---

[16] Williams, W. (2006). The Golden Age of the American Entrepreneur. Hillsdale, MI: Hillsdale College Press.

[17] Meltzer, H. A. (20120. Why Capitalism?. New York, NY: Oxford University Press.

Chapter 3: The Entrepreneur and the Real World

"Thomas Edison, an inventor/entrepreneur, lost almost as much money as he made because of unsuccessful risk-taking."

Jonathan Hughes, 1983

In his landmark book, *Intellectuals and Society*, Thomas Sowell wrote, "Only abstract people in an abstract world are the same."[18] Sowell contended that there are differences between people's knowledge and abilities. The same differences exist between an abstract entrepreneur and the Austrian entrepreneur. The Austrian School of Economics describe the entrepreneur as a subjective individual, their action and economic calculation, and the given consequences of their market action toward profit opportunities. In contrast, the mainstream views the entrepreneur as nonexistent in the grand scheme of market phenomena or as an elusive figure that can just be wiped away as being uninfluential. The Austrian School view the market as an ever-changing interaction of people through spontaneous and harmonious exchange, but through the individual's subjective lens. Only the individual can act to make their situation better, and only customers determine value in an economic good. In the same way, according to the Austrian School, the market equilibrium is an inconceivable market phenomenon being that only isolated persons are in equilibrium.[19] That is because marketplace interaction and exchange is a process, even a discovery process that involves real-world competitors, changing information, and consumer value scales that dictate the production of urgently demanded economic goods. More than that, the Austrian School place emphasis on the fact that entrepreneurs are data changers. Every time a market participant makes a decision, it set forth new points of data that changes the course of future decisions of all

---

[18] Sowell, T. (2012). *Intellectuals and society*. Basic Books, New York, NY.

[19] Hayek, F. A. (1980). *Individualism and Economic Order*. Chicago, IL: University of Chicago Press.

market participants. These notions of the entrepreneur derive from a long line of economists, starting with Carl Menger, who laid the foundation of an Austrian conception of economics and the function of the entrepreneurial in the market process in the book titled, *Principles of Economics*. In the body of Austrian thought major points of interest related to the entrepreneurial function is the importance of knowledge, error, and uncertainty. Austrian economists place a greater emphasis on the function of entrepreneurial awareness of information about changing economic situations. Having this awareness, entrepreneurs are able to make economic calculations, act, and initiate production. An entrepreneur's often-overlooked tool is the function of time, discovery, awareness, and market opportunity. Put together, the entrepreneur is a real person with real aims in a world with real people and changing circumstances; therefore, the entrepreneur has to learn from market experience. There is nothing abstract about the Austrian conception of the entrepreneur. The romanticized entrepreneur does not bear profit, losses; they do not face the consequences of unprofitable decisions. On the contrary, Austrians see the market as a process of flesh-and-blood individual entrepreneurs who seek to make a profit and avoid loss.

Peter Klein noted that the Austrian entrepreneur receives profits because they make better judgments about market conditions.[20] The entrepreneur applies specific knowledge of the market economy to revenue-making opportunities. We live in a world of real people seeking to earn profit and minimize costs. We are not in an abstract world with abstract people, who possess abstract knowledge employed in abstract markets, and who do not face concatenating forces resulting in profit and loss. Only abstract people all have the same knowledge, at the same time, and in the same place. But there is a tendency to romanticize the entrepreneurial process. Often, would-be entrepreneurs assume that since they have the capital and a means of production, customers will rush in to create profits once

---

[20] Klein, P. G. (2010). *The capitalist & the entrepreneur: Essays on organizations & markets*. Auburn, AL: Ludwig von Mises Institute.

a product comes to market. As Sowell said, these are abstract outcomes based on abstract premises. The reality is that entrepreneurs are hemmed in by market constraints such as time and consumer preferences. The entrepreneur is subject to numerous complexities and unforeseen circumstances over which they have no control. While these constraints do not exist in the abstract, in reality, time is of the essence. So, within this constraint, entrepreneurs seek to earn *votes* from customers in the form of their purchases. In the abstract world, entrepreneurs are driven by romantic desires based on what they (abstractly) think consumers want, indeed the abstract entrepreneur possess an omniscient view of what the future holds.

In *Profit and Loss*, Mises stated, "The market is always crammed with visionaries who want to float such impracticable and unworkable schemes."[21] The entrepreneur does not intend to enter a losing situation, but we know that often happens, leading to not-so-romantic outcomes. There is nothing abstract or romantic when consumers cast their votes via money spent on the products or services that meet their expectations. But how does the entrepreneur know the personal, subjective values and desires of customers? The answer is, we do not know, because the future is uncertain.

The most critical fact to consider is that customers dictate market conditions. As Mises noted, entrepreneurs are not rewarded for serving their desires; they are rewarded for serving customers. Profits go to the best provider—the one who can fill the gap between what is and what can be done better. Thinking of entrepreneurial activity in terms of the abstract ignores the importance of consumers' wants, and each consumer is a specific person with specific needs. Knowledge is decentralized, and not all knowledge is equal. Only by understanding specific realities of the marketplace can one profit from existing opportunities. The entrepreneur who moves first has the potential to receive the reward of more significant profit. But acting fast is not enough—one must know what to do to best serve customers. Profits are the result of having good insight and solid

---

[21] von Mises, L. (1951). *Profit and loss*. Auburn, AL: Ludwig von Mises Institute.

judgment. A further reality is that even for those who act both quickly and soundly, there are fast followers (i.e., competitors) who may also serve customers with similar products or services, with losses following for at least some of these entrepreneurs. The real-life approach to entrepreneurship holds that profits are not guaranteed, and losses are common. Indeed, losses are a very unromantic reality that is far from abstract for many entrepreneurs.

Entrepreneurs are necessarily more aware of potential market opportunities than nonentrepreneurs. Precisely because the marketplace does not reflect consistent patterns of preferences. The ability to look outward toward the needs of others with anticipation is the entrepreneur's tool. Everything changes all the time, so entrepreneurs must examine the horizon to determine what lies ahead.[22] To be successful, they must anticipate and recognize every variation in consumer preferences or modifications of needed supplies before their competitors adjust their operations. Entrepreneurs who look at the past for answers to understand the future do not gain the insights required to understand what might be around the corner. While considering past and present data provides information to support decisions about future endeavors—and is useful in many ways to various degrees depending on circumstances—past and present data do not give the full picture of what is ahead, and cannot replace instinct and vision. Peeking around the corner involves observation and gut instinct—putting things together to survive in a continually shifting high-velocity marketplace. If entrepreneurs cannot see what is next or what could be, they are not visionary and may not survive the ups and downs of consumer trends. A person engaged in starting any business must be critically aware of their surroundings to perceive what customers will demand in the context of available resources.

It is difficult to explain why some entrepreneurs who look ahead get it right and move on their intuition despite data that suggest doing otherwise. Most entrepreneurs are resilient and have heard a

---

[22] Kirzner, I. M. (1960). *The economic point of view: An essay in the history of economic thought.* Auburn, AL: Ludwig von Mises Institute.

million times: "No, it can't work!" A prime example is Mary Kay.[23] She was told by many that her ideas to sell cosmetics could not get off the ground, much less succeed. Her husband, her accountant, and a few friends did not understand her vision and instinct. But Mary Kay envisioned and developed a multimillion-dollar organization. This story is similar to that of many other successful entrepreneurs. In Mary Kay's situation, all of the data suggested failure, but her entrepreneurial instincts projected success. I am grateful that many of the successful entrepreneurs ignored the naysayers and pursued vision by following their gut instinct and market trends so we can enjoy the fruits of their vision. Thanks to them, we now have cellphones, high-tech vehicles, and other technologies to make our everyday life easier and more enjoyable.

Another reality of data and information that real entrepreneurs must distill is that in looking ahead, you may see that it is better to imitate what others are doing and mold it into your vision. Even large retailers seek information from other markets, competitors, and industries, realizing innovation is sometimes a product of error and new knowledge, and sometimes of following another firm's ideas. For example, Sears copied General Motors' cost savings methods, then Toyota copied what Sears borrowed from GM, and later Walmart observed that the method used by Sears and GM was effective and adopted it.[24] Consider a yogurt shop. An entrepreneur must look forward and decide how to modify *their* yogurt shop in line with what is coming around the corner—with what will happen next or with what consumers will want next—and customize their shop to those new realities. Then, they will experience success!

---

[23] Ash, K. M. (1981). Mary Kay. New York, NY: Harper & Row

[24] Drucker, P. F. (2009). *Managing in a time of great change.* Boston, MA: Harvard Business Press.

Chapter 4: The Entrepreneur and Competition

"The problem becomes one of how the 'data' of the different individuals on which they base their plans are adjusted to the objective facts of their environment which includes the actions of the other people."[25]

Friedrich A. von Hayek, 1948

Competition in the market economy allows—buyers, sellers, and producers—to improve their economic situation by making decisions on future market discrepancies. Discrepancies between prices, quality, and efficient delivery of products and services are captured by the observing entrepreneur. From a customer perspective, competition drives these decisions that steers consumer choices based on availability, price, quality, and utility. They may also consider whether the seller is in a convenient marketplace or marketspace? On the other hand, the seller (i.e., entrepreneur) make decisions that relate to when to sell a product, how many others are selling the same product, and at what price. A more broad but vital decision might be if it is advantageous for an entrepreneur to enter a market. The decision to enter a market based on the intensity of competition is a vital signal for entrepreneurs.

Most people do not like the word competition, but it has a positive effect on entrepreneurial decision making and consumer choice. At a broader point, Israel Kirzner provided the best definition of competition that can be applied here—"a situation is competitive if no incumbent participant possesses privileges that protect him against the possible entry of new competitors."[26] Moreover, competition is an essential market process that creates favorable conditions, because it determines who and when one can enter a market, innovation, and determines the most urgent uses of

[25] Hayek, A. F. (1948). Individualism and Economic Order. Chicago, IL: The University of Chicago Press

[26] Kirzner, I. M. (2000). The irresistible force of market competition. *Ideas on Liberty*, *50*, 11-16.

resources. Regardless, competition is part of the market process and unveils how best to serve the consumer and affects the going market prices for consumer goods.

As factors of production congeal, there is a spark in production and an increase in capital stock's economic character.[27] Production takes time, but the world is in perpetual motion—it, and the people in it, do not stand still. Buyers and sellers act to satisfy their needs and wants through various means. Because the world and the people in it are not static, there will always be some semblance of competition in a market.

The world is only static to those in a privileged market position. This position of privilege is only granted by satisfied consumers. However, if the world were actually static, there would be no product variation, innovations from viable inventions, price changes, and resources applied to the most urgently demanded economic goods. There would be no profits and no losses. The overall state of market exchanges would be identical. Who wants to sell the same good at the same price and in the same market as their competitor? Fredrick Hayek spoke about competition quite extensively, stating, "the general view seems still to regard the conception of competition currently employed by economists as the significant one and to treat that of the businessman as an abuse."[28]

There are too many differences between people and their approach to what they value the most categorically within consumer goods and services to undervalue the importance of competition. Think of competition this way: each entrepreneur is seeking to gain the same thing within similar timeframes with similar but with nonhomogeneous resources. There are no common denominators in the distribution of consumer value between entrepreneurs. The Austrian conception of the entrepreneur emphasizes the value of

---

[27] Greaves, B. B. (1975). *Free market economics*. Auburn, AL: Ludwig von Mises Institute.

[28] Hayek, F. A. von. (1946). The meaning of competition. *Economic Journal Watch,* 92-106.

competition and how it is a vital function in serving society with want-satisfaction:

- Competition between entrepreneurs *induces innovation* between firms.
- Competition between entrepreneurs *enable cooperation.*
- Competition is a market *process.*
- Competition should allow for *entry.*

Unfortunately, when competition is used in conversation its nature is described in an insidious and war-like tone. Terms such as *tactics*, *take-over*, and *retreat* should not be the words used to describe what is a harmonious market operation. Intuitively, this makes sense; we have grown accustomed to this type of language when we speak of competing and market competition.

Not surprisingly, many incumbent entrepreneurs disdain newcomer competition. Who wants their position shaken by someone with new ideas and innovation that improves the consumers dissatisfaction. Quite often, the newcomer entrepreneur is or can be barred from entering certain markets or industries because of regulations, licensing, permits, and other competitive inducing privileges. The institutional arrangements in a society must be favorable for entrepreneurship to thrive. There are two sides to this coin—potential and existing entrepreneurs are in two different positions and have different aims and visions. Newcomers seek to enter an industry or market where they see opportunity, while existing entrepreneurs have a different vision, one that sees things from a static and stable position. Should the newcomer be barred from entry?

More often than not, there is no temptation to look on the other side of the equation -- a world without competition. A market condition that does not specify a minimum level of competing social cooperation disregards the most important function – the entrepreneur. It takes the creation of market opportunities to increase the number of entrepreneurs, which means innovative will not bubble up to the surface of the marketplace without the efforts of those who can uncover and discover them. There must be a supple environment that entice entrepreneurs with the requisite knowledge to find and close a previous consumer-satisfaction gap. In this sense, and because market and competition is a process, there must be competition to lower consumer costs search based on consumer subjective value scales. However, in these market situations encasing multiple ways of lowering consumers search costs relative to market opportunities, there will be many potential entrepreneurs with keen insights and greater knowledge about any unsatisfied consumer needs and opportunities.

Whether new entrepreneurs can put up their capital resources to attempt to serve the customer better than their competitors deeply depends on the institutional arrangements and economic conditions in which the entrepreneur find themselves operating within. The condition of the market is reflective of the institutional entrepreneurial opportunities available to any one entrepreneur who might reap the benefits of serving the customer better than another entrepreneur.

Entrepreneurs and the entrepreneurial process of discovery modify everyone's knowledge involved in a general market situation and provide more customer value. Each entrepreneur strives against others to find what the customer wants, and under what conditions they are willing to purchase it—using capital to spur positive obsolescence and reinventions of goods and or services based on customer demand. To invoke positive obsolescence is to inject new ideas into the customer's products based on past data reflecting their needs and wants. This injection of positive obsolescence, intended to spur action in consumers, is part of the process of competition between entrepreneurial capitalists and entrepreneurial producers.

There is nothing perfect about the market process of competition, and the knowledge one has at any given time, but we might assume that knowledge is uneven so that competition can produce the knowledge that market participants need to make decisions. While it may sound counterintuitive, (healthy) competition seems to coordinate market activities in ways that noncompetitive mechanisms cannot. Entrepreneurs who have tried and failed, and those who have succeeded in serving customers show that although a newcomer may not get the consumer's vote, customers, and newcomer entrepreneurs are then able to learn the market conditions at a point in time to ascertain whether or not the market will increase their losses or profits. The newcomer's knowledge is shared with the incumbent and helps the incumbent to adjust to new market demands that might otherwise have gone unnoticed.

Again, the world that we live in is not static. The opposite can very well happen; newcomers may shift their resources to the best method and out-compete incumbent entrepreneurs. Some may question how a newcomer with less capital might outperform an incumbent who has a solid market position and an accumulated capital base. There is no fixed answer to this question.

Entrepreneurs must rely on market learning, failing and applying the new knowledge gained from such failure as a guide in the market. The market gives the entrepreneur the desired feedback on success—profit. The incumbent entrepreneur is always adjusting to expectations and market changes whereby they reconcile their capital accumulations. Competition is a coordinating mechanism for entrepreneurs—incumbents and newcomers. Newcomers may enter a market using new ideas and experiences based on the success of incumbent firms. Before newcomers enter markets as a competitor of existing firms, there are many things to consider, such as changes in regulations, price, customers' wants, locations, jobs, and preferences. A newcomer entrepreneur having this knowledge, it would behoove them to utilize market signals, customer dissatisfaction, and newly acquired knowledge at profiting from awareness.

There is a textbook explanation of the nature of market competition, and there is a real-world explanation. Most textbooks state that competition is perfect—but in reality, competition is ever-present, imperfect, and should allow newcomers to try their real-world skills to satisfy customers more efficiently. The question should not be whether more or less competition exists—rather, we should ask who can serve the customer best, or at least better than the other fellow. Which entrepreneur is more efficacious in solving the day-to-day problems that customers all face? Customers like to save both time and money. These two broad and ambiguous factors—time and future events—are the main reason entrepreneurs thrive in the competitive sphere of the market. Competing entrepreneurs can harmoniously apply their knowledge, capital, and skill to seize pure profit opportunities and exploit their resources better than others to decrease consumer dissatisfaction.

In an ideal free or unhampered market, the price mechanism would alert the would-be entrepreneur to the level of profit that might be worth pursuing instead of another profit opportunity altogether. Knowledge is the key component to one's ability to compete for either within an industry or market. Expert knowledge—exclusive to few—can reveal how to alter the cost of production or the cost of services compared with someone who has less knowledge. Unlike some things, knowledge can be upgraded and built upon when it has become obsolete. Many entrepreneurs and small business owners can get locked into an obsolete method of serving the customer. "If it ain't broke, don't fix it," says an adage. But when you know things are broken, adjustments are necessary to serve customers and compete. In some situations, it would not behoove the entrepreneur to switch to better innovative approaches, because consumers will purchase regardless. Maybe so. Some consumers are not fully knowledgeable about what is being offered across the street, and at what price. And the same is true for other entrepreneurs. Competition, for many in business, does not sound like a helpful market process, but it *is* the process that has allowed you a chance at bat! Competition may seem insidious. But as Boorstin said, "It is through competition that the best interests of trade and industry are promoted."[29] In a real way, customers are protected when there is competing forces between various entrepreneurs that enables them to vie for customers using goods and services of good quality offered at the right price.

---

[29] Boorstin, p. 48.

Chapter 5: Entrepreneurship and Culture

"A civilization, we say, is a collection of cultural characteristics and phenomena."[30]

Fernand Braudel, 1982

There are innumerable definitions of the entrepreneur and entrepreneurship, as far as the role entrepreneurs play in a market economy.[31] Still, understandings of place and time are equally important. In many areas around the world, entrepreneurs were historically on the fringe of society. Some of these people belonged to ethnic and ethno-religious groups: Protestants, Calvinists, Baptists, Quakers, and so on. These groups included people who did not fall categorically into the class of craftsmen, mechanics, manufacturers, and traders; rather, they came from families with modest backgrounds. Patterns of entrepreneurial groups can be traced by economic and societal striving for acceptance from industrial enterprises.[32] We know that entrepreneurship has a social origin. In the beginnings of the 17th and 18th centuries, the Americans, English, Japanese, Dutch, Spanish, and French Indians had a common thread of experience pertaining to how entrepreneurial groups were faced with widespread hostility from industry merchants and manufacturers—those who held on to their more obsolete methods of production.

The Huguenot's social standing was indicative of the disdain for entrepreneurial activities in 18th and 19th century Europe.[33] They were townspeople barred from society because of their religious beliefs and cultural attributes. What set this group of people apart

---

[30] Braudel, F. (1982). *On history*. University of Chicago Press.

[31] Hebert, R. F., & Link, A. (2010, June 21). Historical perspectives on the entrepreneur. *Foundations and Trends in Entrepreneurship*, *2*(4).

[32] Bendix, R. (1956). Work and authority in industry. New York: NY. Wiley & Sons, Inc.

[33] Hagen, E. E. (1975). *The economics of development*. Homewood, IL: McGraw-Hill Irwin.

from the rest of French culture is that the greater community considered them native *outsiders*. The Huguenots were accustomed to doing things with their hands, to tinkering, making, and selling their wares to buyers far and near. Another factor is that this group was in no way social or economic elites (in the sense that they controlled capital). Huguenots were looked down upon and went through a time of persecution. For the most part, this cultural group was dissenters from society, but not in terms of their work, innovativeness, and entrepreneurial spirit. What is so striking and telling about the Huguenot entrepreneurial group is that they had "for generations been derogated in its own society—looked down upon unjustly and unreasonably."[34] The Protestants, the Jews, and many other groups have had similar entrepreneurial backgrounds. Historically speaking, entrepreneurs have generally rejected many of society's traditional frameworks through their actions, which, to many, seem unorthodox.

The Chinese, particularly those who migrated to Singapore in the 19th century, dominated the industries and markets of Singapore not long after their arrival. This select group had long developed the tradition of private property and business acumen needed to adapt their capitalism in other parts of the world, mainly Southeast Asia (Taiwan, Indonesia, and Hong Kong). The Chinese who arrived in Singapore were people forced out of mainland China during the Manchu Dynasty. They migrated to Singapore to find a better life and escape poverty.[35] They used the business skills they had acquired in China through the family business unit and applied the same skills to businesses in their new land.

It is easy to see a connection between entrepreneurial behaviors, imperatives, and decision making that is embedded within the cultural framework. Culture of any sort speaks of the norms and experiences one has encountered in life. Whichever cultural group one belongs to, there is an assumption of shared ideas and a

---

[34] Hagen, E. E. (1975). *The economics of development.*

[35] Clive, L. (2019). *Chinese entrepreneurship in Singapore: History, Faith & Culture.* Midview City, Singapore: Graceworks Private Limited.

particular value system permeating the individual's everyday life and society. The cultural links to entrepreneurship entail working toward a personal state of intrinsic satisfaction, or helping others by creating something novel. For some, entrepreneurship is a form of religious expression that leads to a closer connection with God; in the long-run, believers will receive salvation.[36] Many factors can connect with culture, such as religion, work ethic, a sense of purpose, previous familial business, a sense of intellectual enlightenment, and perhaps once lived in a region that cultivated entrepreneurship and small business owners.

A culture that has matured over time through experiences reaps the benefits of that accumulated experience and knowledge in the form of entrepreneurs and small business owners. As we know them today, the caricature of the entrepreneur is rooted in the ways of the Yankee peddler. The New England peddler traveled across the country selling forks, spoons, and knives—various wares—to families in coastal and remote villages on foot and later on wagons.[37] These were ambitious and rugged individuals who supplied customers both far and near. They were cobblers, grinders, gunsmiths, clockmakers, steel producers, vehicle manufacturers, and on and on. Many industries formed from the strong culture of self-ownership in earlier times. It was the need for peddlers to travel long distances that created roads, which led to the development of the horse and carriage, first as the one-horse chaise, and eventually leading to the development of railroads and eventually to the mass production of vehicles.

Not all societies enthusiastically share this culture of business and market activity. The motivating factor imputed to entrepreneurship culture has been making money and profit through means that are less than desirable. Throughout time, the connotation of market exchange and profit has changed in many regards. In particular, one is that now we recognize the tremendous motivating

---

[36] Weber, M. (1958). *The Protestant ethic and the spirit of capitalism: And other writings*. New York, NY: Scribner's Sons.

[37] Boorstin, D. J. (1965). *The Americans: The national experience.* New York, NY: Random House.

factors that encourage one to pursue a lifestyle of entrepreneurship. Self-discipline and valuing one's life and work come together to form the vision and motivation to pursue something as risky as entrepreneurship. Another point often overlooked is the fulfillment of learning from other cultures and being receptive to learning new things from other people. Simply put, if you only spend a couple of hours on your business and observe that competing business owners are spending up to 30 hours a week on their business, there will be a big difference in the outcome dependent upon your action of that observation. Again, there is a benefit to learning from the market as it provides market participants signals and directions that enhances decision making. Learning in a community from others who share a similar mindset and goal in life is advantageous to the entrepreneur for human capital development; however, in a market economy entrepreneurs also learn from others whom they do not share any commonality other than the products or services they deem important and who should provide these products and services and at what price.

Historically, some groups of people or even regions where a group of people shared similar and dissimilar skill sets allowed for the exchange of goods by the barter system, which accelerated the likelihood of entrepreneurship. Such exchanges accelerated the use of money paper and coins to replace the lingering, inefficient, and often inaccurate barter system.

Over the last decade, the understanding and definition of entrepreneurship has changed many times over. This change is neither good nor bad, but it has occurred in terms of technology, access to credit, knowledge, availability of information, and overall lifestyle choices. The ideology of entrepreneurs still has ties to the past. However, today people thinking of pursuing entrepreneurship can choose to serve customers using their capital or work for an employer. Culture and productivity may have a few connections. No civilization has ever existed that was not productive in some way. Productive in the sense that they were able to trade with other people who were able to produce those things that were of higher value than what they previously had. Productivity, in any sense of the word, allows for the flourishing of human energy. Productivity is the cornerstone of any market economy.

Productivity can be both intellectual and of a physical manifestation. Some people have written poems, music, or made physical products that people can enjoy. Productivity allows everyone to become better off than they were before the act of production for the purpose for someone else; pursuit of one's goals can only happen when productive. However, individuals cannot pursue their goals unless other market participants are equally productive. Productive and unproductive individuals have one thing in common: they both consume economic goods produced by themselves or other people. What I mean here is that the power of productivity is far-reaching. Most of those reading this are thinking about productivity in several ways. In short, though, consider that someone must make, package, and sell an item or offer a service for someone else to purchase. When you buy a product, you have essentially earned the claim on that purchase, and thus you are then able to make another purchase. If farmers and grocers were absent from the marketplace to provide and sell me food, I would go hungry, and I would be unproductive in my contributions to society and in the marketplace for someone else to be productive. Mises provides us with a clear example:

the inhabitants of the Swiss Jura prefer to manufacture watches instead of growing wheat. Watchmaking is for them the cheapest way to acquire wheat. On the other hand, the growing of wheat is the cheapest way for the Canadian farmer to acquire watches....tailors do not make their own shoes and shoemakers do not make their own clothes.[38]

---

[38] von Mises, L. (1988). *Human action: A treatise on economics*. Auburn, AL: Ludwig von Mises Institute.

Chapter 6: Entrepreneurial Usefulness or Uselessness

"Basic question: What did Rockefeller supply to others that caused so many of those to turn their own individually modest sums of money over to him, adding up to his vast fortune?"[39]

Thomas Sowell, 2016

There are innumerable instances where products and services were bought and produced for customers that were later found to be useless, with no consumer utility. The market determines the usefulness or uselessness of products. There are numerous instances where the free market was at work in identifying products that were not useful in their current state and needed improvement to be useful to customers: the cassette tape and Napster, the McDonalds Arch Deluxe sandwich, telephone, and the coffee maker. During the production of these products, they were deemed useful to customers. Over time, however, they either lost their usefulness or were replaced by newer or better products. Time is a primary factor in usefulness and uselessness.

Speaking of time and usefulness, during the 17th century, people would purchase clocks from peddlers without knowing how to tell time.[40] The paradox is that the clock was useful in a subjective sense, but it was not in a practical sense to these people who were unable to tell time from a clock. To the entrepreneur, an initial idea may be considered useful at one point, but time lapses and circumstances change. Eventually, through the passing of time, the entrepreneur will experience a loss or a profit.

Similarly, customers use products that have utility; over time, customers are discontent and demand more valued product features. If the product or service alters, the customer may become

---

[39] Sowell, T. (2016). *Wealth, poverty and politics*. Basic Books, New York, NY.
[40] Dolan, J. R. (1964). *The Yankee peddlers of early America*. New York, NY: CN Potter.

dissatisfied. Dissatisfaction results from the dissonance a customer experiences when they cannot satisfactorily use, control, and rank the importance of a product or service. The entrepreneur cannot think linearly when it comes to the link between what they want to produce and bring to the marketplace and consumers' values. An entrepreneur may think that because they have resources, production equipment, and can get a product to market, they will satisfy customers' needs. It is the opposite approach that works best in terms of the delivery of valuable goods—one that first considers the customer, then the importance of the product/service, and only *then* production.

There are times, however, when the entrepreneur gets it right. They see things correctly not only in terms of calculating the capital investment needed, maintaining a low cost of production, and fashioning the right mix of advertising and marketing for their product or service. No one experiences a loss if an economic good brought to market is deemed useless by market participants except the entrepreneur, a fortiori to earn the residual profit. The entrepreneurial paradox has always been profit or loss—all based on an idea of what may have seemed like a great product or service but was not appreciated by market participants.

On the surface, this may seem intuitive—the customer likes a product and, of course, will buy it. If they don't value it or find utility for it, they won't buy it. As easy as this sounds, the more complicated idea is where value emerges to the customer. Never mind the resources used to create the product or offer the service. These production factors have extraordinarily little to do with what is involved in the final product rising or falling on the customer's value scale. This is behind the saying "think like the customer," because that is the first way to identify if a product or service will be useless. One has to ask: How important is this good to the customer? How dependent is the customer on the service that I want to offer people? Answers to these questions are critical to determine how sustainable and long-lasting a business idea will be.

I often ponder but have yet to find an answer: Why would an entrepreneur bring a useless product or a service to a market?

Perhaps it is not intentional. However, I think about the common saying that most businesses fail in the first five years. It could be a case where the entrepreneur saw something within their vision and judged that it would be profitable to use their resources elsewhere or perhaps they had the foresight to anticipate customers' future wants and needs. Either way, we can infer the entrepreneur lacked knowledge or misinterpreted some signals or shifts in the market. I can understand how entrepreneurs want to go into a business that is comfortable and easy to do given an experienced background in that particular industry. The fact is that if it's easy for you, then it's easy for someone else to acquire the same supplies or offer the same or similar service in any unfettered market environment. This is not a bad situation, but it is the nature of competition, which should not hinder competition but signal others to follow.

The other essential type of entrepreneur is the entrepreneur-capitalist. The entrepreneur-capitalist invests in production, purchases the necessary land, and obtains any other raw resources needed to bring goods to production. They supply the money needed or acquire existing businesses. These entrepreneurs put their money into capital goods that do not deliver instant results—these investments often take time to design and produce to earn a profit. Such entrepreneurs invest their money factors into production with the hopes of a future return. They, too, are at the mercy of the real world, which is in constant flux and where time is finite. The timing of entering a market is much more sensitive at predicting whether a product will be useless or useful.

Profitability directly determines a product or service's usefulness. An entrepreneur's longevity also determines usefulness in the market. Entrepreneurs today have it much easier than the entrepreneurs in the dawn of the 17th century. Today's technology and software systems allow entrepreneurs to reach markets across the globe at the push of a keyboard button, which enables just about anyone to start some kind of business. Even countries that do not have bandwidth can pursue entrepreneurial opportunities. Industries can be created through institutional arrangements or become obsolete as a result of consumer demonstrated preferences. Many industries may never become obsolete, as long as they are responsive to customers and find new and appropriate ways to produce valuable goods.

There are many examples of start-ups that immediately provided valuable goods to customers and maintained long-term market vitality. The Mary Kay cosmetics line started out bootstrapping and eventually succeeded as a significant cosmetic industry player. Since then, there have been many competitors. Mary Kay products could one day become obsolete—but this has not yet been the case, because their products are demonstrated by consumers to be useful.

A similar situation occurred with a small upstart called Dalsey, Hillblom and Lynn, commonly known as DSL—a transport and logistical firm started from meager beginnings[41]. DSL found a niche in the transport services industry and has been around ever since. Their usefulness was not so much in what they were providing but how and where they provided their useful service. If Mary Kay and DHL were mere dog-and-pony shows, they would have lost their usefulness long ago. The beautiful thing about entrepreneurship and the market process is that no single person can determine how useful or useless an idea will be. The customer's mind determines useful or uselessness—not anyone else.

The peddlers who sold clocks to villagers knew they did not understand time, nor was telling time necessary until the railroads started running through the villages on schedules. Far from the days of the New England peddler, many start-ups, bootstrappers, and investors can now use multiple platforms and software to assist in determining the usability of ideas for new investments based on the extent their ideas, which may have a long-lasting impact and gain acceptance by potential customers.

Technology, transportation, and social platforms allow entrepreneurs to access potential customers in distant markets. In contrast, having access to marketing tools and employing them in various markets does not guarantee the products or offerings will be

---

[41] Chung, P., & Bowie, R. (2017). *DHL: From startup to global upstart*. Berlin, Germany: Walter de Gruyter.

useful to the customers most urgent needs. Advertising has been around for centuries in different forms, but remains a crucial method to educate potential customers. While past entrepreneurs were not marketing in the sense we understand now, advertising has been around for some time and can be the entrepreneurs' best tool. Advertising provides and extends information to people who ultimately act on it. Advertising is not arbitrary—it should direct, target, and in many cases, educate customers for the long term. While short-term advertising is useful in many ways, it can be costly. The goal is longevity of the brand position. If people with specific household tasks do not have the latest information on a particular product, how would they know where to purchase it and how its performance compares to competing products? New information compounded with existing information helps customers determine a product's usefulness or uselessness in application. The Swiffer is an excellent example of the entrepreneurial paradox between useless and useful.[42] Marketability, absorbing customer interactions, and continuous iterations of the product created Swiffer's especially useful home cleaning products. Nascent entrepreneurs might ask themselves is their product or service useful or useless for consumers future consumption? We see a familiar pattern—the customer at the center of the market—driving entrepreneurs to innovate useful products and service offerings. For example, rubber was around for centuries, but with increase commercial use Harvey Firestone befriended Henry Ford who was at the cusp of the mass production of automotive vehicles. The rubber instantly become useful and a resource to be used for the production of an in-demand product – the vehicle. Firestone, the entrepreneur, understood the uselessness of his rubber resource only used for bicycle manufacturing and ran into an innovation dilemma, which was how to keep the tire on the vehicle rim in place, obviously keeping the rubber tire on the rim of the vehicle was a big deal and required skill and entrepreneurial thinking. Firestone was

---

[42] West, H. (2014). A chain of innovation: The creation of Swiffer. *Research-Technology Management*, *57*(3), 20-2.

determined to find ways to maintain usefulness of the rubber resources he had toward serving customers who were yet to purchase their first vehicle.

Useful products and services cannot emerge out of the thin air. Entrepreneurial alertness requires an individual to observe changing situations and to notice that somewhere, somehow, another entrepreneur made a mistake offering a product or service that was useless at a particular time, recognizing this, and recreating the useless product into something useful. It is the epitome of entrepreneurial thinking—how to take a long-forgotten or a relatively unused product or service and make it relevant today!

Chapter 7: Entrepreneurship and Value

"As a rule, medieval scholars were not interested in machines, but the clock, because of its connection with astronomy, was an exception."[43]

Carlo M. Cipolla, 1968

What is value? How is it measured? Value is the cornerstone of all entrepreneurial endeavors. The term *value* is ambiguous in the business vernacular because value is typically thought of as something embedded in the production of products or service offerings. Value is seen only through the eyes of the consumer and how high or low the value means to them at a particular point in time. There is, however, a link between entrepreneurship and customer's value scale. What does the entrepreneur produce, sell, or invest in that consumers sense is valuable? Consumers' value perception is the baseline for this question. If entrepreneurs do not focus on what the consumer perceives as value, they are likely to miss the mark, leading to loss and a lack of sustainability. Product ingredients do not transmit value; a product or service does not have value built into it. There is no greater or lesser value in a product or service based on the time and uniqueness added when produced—which is a challenging idea for many beginners to understand. Understanding the human mind and perception is almost impossible, if not impractical, due to the time and energy involved in such a pursuit. Entrepreneurs must focus on the consumer and satisfying their needs and acknowledge the ever-challenging nature of value. Instead of thinking, "what do I have to bring to market?", think, "what can I do for customers that they perceive are essential to their personal goals?"

There is a wide disparity between customers' needs and wants and what they deem important (e.g., toilet paper, ice cream, clothing,

---

[43] Cipolla, C. M. (2003). *Clocks and culture, 1300-1700*. WW Norton & Company.

and food). If we take these examples and rank them categorically by importance, we come up with *our* ranking, not that of our customers. We can ask the customer, but then it would only be that individual customer's ranking and not representative of all customers across the globe. We know that customers like to be satisfied, and acquire goods when they need or want them.

The first and essential understanding of value is that it derives from customers' valuation. Outside of what entrepreneurs may think about their products and services, customers decide what is valuable, and to what extent. A product has many features and benefits. These features and benefits, produced and incrementally amended throughout the production cycle, are added improvements for the product's buyer which is the result of changing preferences and the innovation process both meeting at an intersection of the inevitable market process. The market process and innovation and recombination of product resources takes time. For nontangible products, such as a service is adjusted based on customer feedback. If you an apple seller in a storefront has an array of delicious apples ready for sale, the customer determines the importance and value of those apples only at that moment in time. The apple seller does not know which apple (and at which time) is more valuable to customers until a customer makes a purchase. The apple seller might see which type of apple buyers purchase and which they do not. If the apple seller asks each customer a question about which apple they value the most, each customer will probably give a different answer, and perhaps an entirely different answer on a different day of the week.

There is no slam dunk if one grasp what might appear (to you) to be a trend, because trends, by definition, change over time. The Achilles heel of the entrepreneur—change. The importance of goods changes over time. For example, if an employee on her way to work did not pack her lunch, and a nice-looking fruit stand across from her place of work offers a variety of fruit for sale, the apple or orange offered becomes needed and valuable. She would rather have an apple than nothing. However, if you asked the same customer if she would be willing to buy the apple if she had already packed a lunch, the apple would not be as valuable to her—though not because the apple is lousy or she does not like apples. It is merely that the time and place affect the assigned level of importance and value.

What customers know also plays an essential part in determining what they deem is valuable. There may be other apple stands nearby, selling other apples of better quality and at a better price. Here, we lack knowledge in two areas: what the entrepreneur knows and what the customer knows. It is the knowledge problem that will persist for as long as customers seek to satisfy their needs. Needs are a driving force and should be considered by entrepreneurs who have an idea but are not sure if it is the right endeavor. Think about need, dependence, and importance. Some goods and services have always existed—and always will—because people depend on them to conduct their lives.

"You have to start somewhere" is the common cliché, but the saying is a means to express that anyone can and should attempt getting their business idea off the ground. While experience is a great tool to have, and can be assumed to add to one's success, there is something about naivety that can propel you to do something different. There are many perspectives on an entrepreneur's lack of experience in not having done something before and deciding to do it and give it a try. Naivety in this context means a lack of experience, but too often, articles and books speak mostly from the practitioner's perspective and seldom speak to those who are entirely inexperienced when it comes to starting from scratch—bootstrapping. However, some of the best inventions, innovations, and long-lasting companies have been discovered by people who had no previous experience in a particular field.

Using the example of Mary Kay again, I can note that she had no real background in women's cosmetics and yet went on to create the world's most successful women's cosmetics brand. The same might be said for Wallace Calvin Abbott, the creator of Abbott Laboratories. He did not have a background in that area of pharmacology, but he held steadfast despite a changing medical landscape. He found greater opportunity at the time by sending helpful tips and best practices, i.e. marketing, to medical practitioners on useful pharmaceutical methods and practices.[44] Inexperience can go a long way—all entrepreneurs had to start somewhere and without experience.

The caveat with possessing little to no experience is that it presumes risk. Remember, profit and loss can be purely psychological. When attempting to act in the marketplace as an entrepreneur, the primary question should be whether or not the current situation will become better after acting rather than if action had never taken place? It is that fact that all entrepreneurs started from a state of limited knowledge of the market works and the most effective use of resources to satisfy consumers want-satisfactions. Risk is cognitive, which is not to say that there is never objective, tangible loss. Knowingly or unknowingly, entrepreneurs without experience can venture into the unknown by acting on their subjective ends using their means of production. Entrepreneurs with little to no experience can find ways to use their capital to increase their market value. Action attempts to make better future circumstances using available resources and within favorable institutional arrangements. Action despite little to no previous experience is the mark of the entrepreneur and essential to their role in an economy.

Inexperienced entrepreneurs have discovered and adjusted several industries and developed new markets for products and services in innumerable ways. One may have experience making a particular product; that same skill may be the key to creating a process improvement in another industry. Historically, it was naivety that caused innovation and the coupling of industries. The growing field of communications brought together the means to enable mass production, mass transportation,[45] and mass distribution that exploded modern retail's capacity to reach the masses. Out of naivety, from an entrepreneurial perspective, nonexperience regarding a particular action should and ought to be

---

[44] Kogan, H. (1963). *The long white line: The story of Abbott Laboratories*. New York, NY: Random House.

[45] Chandler, A. D., Jr. (1993). *The visible hand*. Cambridge, MA: Harvard University Press.

viewed positively allowing the use not only of fresh, but *different* eyes to examine market errors. New ideas are market-tested, pursued, or cross-pollinated to form new or better goods and services because of entrepreneurial inexperience. Eli Whitney, the innovator who created replaceable parts, had little experience. Because of the creation of replaceable parts, he could assist in forging other industries related to vehicle mass production and arms manufacturing.[46] Daniel Boorstin said, "It is significant that Whitney was inexperienced in making guns. He had probably never carefully examined the particular Charleville musket he contracted to reproduce."[47]

In the 19th century, the ice packaging and shipping industry was created by two entrepreneurs who knew absolutely nothing about shipping ice so that it remained in a frozen block until it arrived at its destination. Not only did they find ways to ship ice as far as India—still frozen—they also created a system to transport ice by the ton from pond to dock for mass transport across the globe. The astute reader might ask: Why would businesses in India and Brazil purchase frozen water from two New Englanders? This question gets back to the central theme of this chapter—the consumer determines value. Experience is a collection of knowledge. If used correctly, knowledge can have long-term positive results. Naivety and the inexperience of entrepreneurs cannot be overlooked or underestimated. Many products and services—and sometimes whole industries—have been the result of inexperience. Countries have flourished because of their lack of experience. They simply did not know any better—there were no pre-established industry structures to constrain human energy in any particular direction. The social framework for newness and a lack of preconceived notions of social power brought brings in tremendous amounts of innovation.[48]

---

[46] Boorstin, D. J. (1965). *The Americans: The national experience.* New York, NY: Random House.
[47] Chamberlain, J. (1976). *The roots of capitalism.* North Shadeland, IN Liberty Fund.
[48] Ibid., p. 32.

Whether an entrepreneur is experienced or inexperienced, they can produce something in which a customer finds value.

Chapter 8: Entrepreneurship and Markets

"It stands to reason that sellers and buyers cannot gather together at certain times and places without an attraction or an interest which compensates for or which even exceeds the expenses of the journey and of the transportation of the produce and merchandise. Without this attraction, each would remain home."[49]

Anne Robert Jacques Turgot, 1757

It was said that "the big invention was not the Model T but the market for the Model T."[50] Most people who aspire to be in business or are in business understand what a market and all of its components are. Traditional business and economics have let us know that a market is where buyers and sellers make exchanges under certain conditions. The buyer can accept the offer of a seller or reject it and move along to the next good option available to them. However, this does not fully explain what a market is and why the entrepreneur should understand it.

The market acts as a process. On an ongoing basis, market attitudes tend to change; as things change in the market, prices react. Particularly in a free market, unfettered products and services are traded according to the customer's willingness and ability to pay market prices.[51] The question is, who are the buyers and what price are they willing to pay for the perceived value? The market resembles relationships—relationships between market participants and decision making, prices, and institutions. Such a process creates circumstances that entrepreneurs must recognize as they emerge. The entrepreneur is always at the whim of the market process and the many decisions (made for various reasons) that coincide with or destroy an entrepreneur's opportunity. Entrepreneurs either adjust

---

[49] Turgot, J. R. A. (2011). The Turgot Collection: Writings, Speeches and Letters of Anne Robert Jacques Turgot. Auburn, AL: LvMI Mises Institute.

[50] Cohen, R. (2006). *Sweet and low: A family story*. New York, NY: Macmillan.

[51] Baetjer, H., Jr. (2017). *Economics and free markets: A Reader*. Washington, DC: Cato Institute.

their costs and price structure to match the market or move to another market.

Most people misunderstand entrepreneurship because they believe the endeavor as describing what the entrepreneurship wishes to make, produce, or bring to market. This is an incorrect understanding of what it means to be an entrepreneur or a purveyor of value to people. Markets comprise buyers, sellers, and producers seeking to make each other better off than they were before. The market allows for these people to interact and coordinate their plans through relationships and market responses.[52] Each individual is willing to exchange what they value least for something they value more. While this is not a shocking lesson, it is a unique insight that must be comprehended—that entrepreneurship requires understanding or having the foresight to know what others value the most and, more importantly, the least. The consumer sees the value that is inherent in what the seller provides. Entrepreneurial exchanges trade for other participants in market value, and economic goods exchange in markets for the sake of other economic goods. While money is involved, it is only the medium that enables the value exchange.[53]

Customers buy goods based on their perceived valuation and utility. They buy things that are useful to them—not those that are useless to them. Even on the decreasing margin of utility, the last unit is still useful if the good is somewhere high enough on the customer's value scale. The market brings useful items (subjectively) to buyers and disregards items that are not. The caveat is that this process ought to protect not the entrepreneur but the customer.

People come together because they value something that someone else does not. Entrepreneurs are the purveyors of goods to buyers, while buyers are the purveyors of information. Both information and highly valued goods are used as consumer and entrepreneurial tools in market ecosystems. Entrepreneurs

---

[52] Chamberlain.

[53] von Mises. (1988). *Human action.*

acknowledge a return on their investment for bringing goods to market, but could only do so due to the consumer information given to them. Furthermore, the consumer has highly valued goods because the entrepreneur brought them to market under better exchange conditions than another seller. The entrepreneur is part of society and, as such, is dependent on society. Society, to the acting entrepreneur, is the combination of individuals cooperating to fulfill each other's needs.[54]

The term market conditions, and its normal connotation should be understood to refer to more than a physical or cloud location. For instance, in our current time there are more robust communication devices and lower transportation costs than ever before. These factors allow entrepreneurs to exchange at a faster rate, and to respond to needs beyond their physical location. The institutions in which society operate consists of private property, markets, language, culture, competition, and social cooperation. These institutions enhance and or modify the conditions in which entrepreneurs' discovery takes place and harness opportunities appear. Markets are, in many cases, ubiquitous, and interconnected within and between industries and other regional markets. Markets are omnipresent and exist anywhere that people meet or can be connected with via technological devices.

Markets allow the entrepreneur to operate omnichannel—in as many places as feasible. However, this may not always be economically practicable. To a large degree, entrepreneurship is thinking of the unfeasible and making it feasible initially through a vision and later in action. This vision is what the entrepreneur sees that no one else can see. The market and its movements work as a malleable set of circumstances that do not stand still but are constantly adjusting to resource levels, prices, and consumer demands. These changes are why entrepreneurship is difficult.

The market only provides customers those things that are useful and not useless at a particular price. Customers make personal choices for the products and services that are important to them and

---

[54] Ibid., p. 143.

fulfill their satisfaction-wants. However, many seek a place in the market as an entrepreneur without understanding this critical fact. To sustain the market process, the entrepreneur must compete for markets and adapt to changing market conditions that may or may not be favorable given to what they have decided to bring to market.

It is instructive that there is a distinction between competitive and noncompetitive markets. When we think of competitive markets, there is a sense of many providers or entrepreneurs, and that the barriers to entry to a particular industry are low (i.e., cost of business tools and machinery). There is often a noticeable difference in a competitive market, where prices are at or near the market level. Competitive markets are highly transitory than non-competitive markets. The same is true with the price of labor. In competitive markets, labor price tends to be, on net balance, lower than in noncompetitive markets, where labor tends to be specialized and require expert knowledge. Nonspecialized knowledge is the only requirement other than capital in noncompetitive markets. Noncompetitive markets tend to have entrepreneurs compete at lower prices, vying with competing entrepreneurs based on quality.

The main difference is what is needed for the entrepreneur to enter a market as a newcomer. What are the prerequisites to bring a level of human capital to an economic environment? In the scope of basic entrepreneurship, the more competitive a market is in comparison to others that have higher barriers to entry, the easier it is for entrepreneurs to enter for the short run. This freedom of entry shapes entrepreneurs' market offerings and the extent to which they can remain in an industry without experiencing long-run losses. On the other hand, noncompetitive markets are environments with large amounts of expert knowledge and long-term market position that require outsiders to overcome many barriers before they can enter to compete. Alternatively, the would-be entrepreneur may not have the capital to pursue an idea in a competitive market because the knowledge circulating may be incomprehensible to a newcomer without the possessing expert knowledge. Some noncompetitive industries are increasingly difficult to acquire and find capital for one to enter and survive in the long term, due to the high levels of investment that it would take to spur market activity.

In any given market, in addition to customers, there are numerous people and institutions involved—small firms, large firms, corporations, governments, nonprofits, legal, and the like that coordinating market participants plans. It is up to the entrepreneur to decide what industry they are best suited, and to understand the players in that industry's market. This is not clear-cut; some industries have multiple markets (e.g., health care). Even freelance marketers will have multiple markets in which they might conduct their business. While a small start-up financial firm will serve multiple markets, it may not serve all of them well, because markets are fluid, not static.

The production of sugar was first recorded in Geoffrey Chaucer's *The Canterbury Tales* in 1387. King Henry III claimed sugar to be a special item to procure in 1226 because of the demand by customers who found the taste and use to be fulfilling. Even William Shakespeare mentioned sugar several times in his plays.[55] In the early 1950s, three major shifts in the change in the tastes and preferences of people allowed Eisenstadt to create Sweet'N Low, a sugar substitute. He did not create the sugar market, but he took advantage of three trends to create a market for Sweet'N Low: dieting, sanitary restaurants and utensils, and diabetics in need of an alternative sweetener.

Sweet'N Low was originally launched and sold at A&P supermarkets and primarily promoted as a medicine and dietary aid for people with diabetes. Eventually, a broader group of people enjoyed not the purported medicinal purposes of Sweet'N Low but its ability to sweeten beverages and foods. It eventually became a common product in many households. Other market factors added to the favorability of Sweet'N Low, which was market signals for Eisenstadt: the diet craze, the common use of bathroom scales, diet soft drinks, and a more health-conscious generation. The market

---

[55] Macinnis, P. (2002). *Bittersweet: The story of sugar*. Crows Nest, Australia: Allen & Unwin.

trend was on his side when he and his wife sat down at the dinner to eat and noticed an empty bowl of sugar on the counter. The open sugar bowl on the dinner counter immediately struck him as a product packaged for the individual – an individual pack of sugar – was what he discovered and found a market for customers who prefer to have their individualized sugar packets.

When markets are free to enter, that is, when people discover new ideas and compete with others to fulfill the needs and wants of their fellows, it not only provides entrepreneurs and customers a way to coordinate their plans, but does so for society as a whole. Try to imagine the world without entrepreneurs. It is not easy to do, because we will always have needs to fulfill. There has always been, and there will always be entrepreneurship. Did entrepreneurs emerge because there was a market for them, or did they emerge because there was no market for them to use their skill and human energy to serve others? It is a question for the ages, but one that we could ponder forever.

There is little evidence that a group of people created the market by sitting around and deciding its plans and design. The market process is a remarkable phenomenon created and designed by buyers and sellers seeking to make their situation better. The market, it is true, is a mechanism that allows individuals to find what they can uniquely provide or what they possess best in the productive sphere to serve others. What other social arrangement allows distant groups of people to find products or services other than a harmonious market process that incorporates freedom of entry of those who have means to pursue profitable discoveries through social exchange. The needs of customers and their willingness to buy via a price is a signal to individuals and groups of individuals who seek to dive deeply into a craft that benefits others, because prices brings awareness to consumers most urgent needs, limited or abundant supply of resources, and or a growing or lagging market. With that, there is more of a variety of degrees of competitiveness in some markets than in others. The upside is the market does not show profitable signals where the likelihood of survival is limited, and resources are unavailable, which deters individuals from entry and malinvestment.

It is easy to see the compassion that has emerged through the market process in human development. The market has opened doors for people to do things for others, and in many ways, created conditions for humanity to flourish. Of course, nothing is perfect, and humans are not omniscient or omnipotent. While the market and its processes are not panaceas for societal ills and problems, it does allow individuals to use their resources to address them if they choose. In a market system, unlike other economic systems, people are bound together by "mutual dependence."[56] This mutual dependence manifests itself in exchange environments where individuals can serve others most efficiently, and at the same time, individual preferences can reveal themselves by choices made. People's choices are subjective and made toward future action, and it is the entrepreneur who plays the vital role of coordinating these market activities in response to consumer subjective valuations.

---

[56] Ekelund, B. R., Hebert, F. R. (1983). A History of Economic Theory and Method. NY, New York: McGraw-Hill.

Chapter 9: The Entrepreneur and Market Conditions

"In 1756, when Watt applied to the city of Glasgow for the right to open a workshop, the trade corporations, invoking their medieval privileges, objected."[57]

John Chamberlain, 1976

Economic conditions and opportunities arise from errors that others make or from drastic changes in market conditions. Errors discovered by entrepreneurs in a marketplace affects how market participants make decisions. Entrepreneurs learn from and listen to market participants' perceptions, and dissatisfactions. Error is a gift to the entrepreneur, especially the newcomer. Errors allow entrepreneurs to do something better than an incumbent entrepreneur. Error adjustment can occur either in thinking, use of technology, or choices. No one willingly operates in error, as they have adverse effects. Indeed, one always acts purposefully to pursue better conditions for oneself.

What is error? One is in error when influences outside of one's control have changed without being recognized. If one person is selling an item for $10, and another person is selling it for $3, someone is in error. If customers are dissatisfied, and the entrepreneur continues to miss or ignore opportunities to reverse their dissatisfaction, they are in error. If a seller misses an opportune time to make product adjustments, they have missed the trial by error.

When information and knowledge between market participants are disproportionate, individuals must choose between options that may or may not be part of their end goal. Entrepreneurs act purposefully, as Mises stated in *Human Action*,[58] and they use their insight of the best use of their resource to find ways to adjust by trial

---

[57] Chamberlain, J. (1959). The Roots of Capitalism. Indianapolis, ID: Liberty Press.

[58] von Mises, L. (1998). *Human action: A treatise on economics*. Indianapolis, IN Liberty Fund, Inc.

and error. The entrepreneur never fixes the error, only adjusts it to eliminate customer dissatisfaction. Because the entrepreneur must discern the real economic conditions, the next best option for many is to revert to previously missed opportunities to adjust. Trial by error is the process of reasoning and thinking that understands the market is not frozen and attempts as many product and service adjustments as are needed in real time.

The question of error is self-explanatory. Humans are fallible, not omniscient, or omnipotent. Thus, we must use error to learn and adjust. It is highly possible that people will pursue aims or market options that were not part of their initial goals under various economic conditions. This is a good thing for an entrepreneur. Schumpeter coined a term to signify this phenomenon—*creative destruction*.[59] Creative destruction preempts market errors.

Most, if not all, actions of entrepreneurs with knowledge about market conditions are based on customer dissatisfaction. For example, an ice cream shop owner may or may not be privy to the high unemployment rates of a given year; at the same time, they may not see how unemployment rates and market prices will influence their business. Entrepreneurs adjust any undesirable behavior to more desirable and satisfactory behavior—not for themselves but their customers. The ice cream shop owner must acknowledge any errors and adjust their business offerings. A webmaster entrepreneur has been using a specific tool to build webpages only to discover their tools are not changing their clients' dissatisfaction with their web pages. That entrepreneur has been inefficient in the market and is in error, because they are unaware of the tools needed to create satisfaction and has not adjusted the error of opportunity to create more satisfaction for the client.

Alchian and Allen (2018) agreed that entrepreneurs think of new ideas and investigate them "in the hope of finding profitable products or methods of production and distribution."[60] There tends

---

[59] Schumpeter, J. (1942). *Capitalism, socialism, and democracy*. New York, NY: Harper and Row.
[60] Armen, A. A, & Allen, R. W. (2018). *Universal economics*. Carmel, IN Liberty Fund.

to be objection to the opportunity of error, or to a limiting of errors, but I argue that improvements and opportunities (i.e., "gold") are within these errors.

Many seek to avoid errors and achieve efficiency. But the entrepreneur must embrace errors and adapt to market shifts and exchange conditions. Errors in forecast and judgement can go undetected by the unaware entrepreneur —indeed, the ice cream shop owner might have made some connections between their shop and unemployment within the region and its relation to potential employees. They should also consider whether or not market participants in the region will limit outings for ice cream because of their shrinking disposable income due to unemployment. How can the owner be more efficient in that market, adjust their offerings, and harness opportunities?

There will always be a need for trial and error in a market process as people try to coordinate plans based on an unknown future. When pursuing entrepreneurial goals, one is prone to making some mistakes. Knowledge and data of the specific situation and communication with customers and networks of what is happening is the mechanism to ensure opportunities—entrepreneurial knowledge composed of not only the primary business operations but in the market process in general. There are always two possible prices for the same product and service and quality differentials between similar products and services; it is the entrepreneur's job to find these differences and translate them into opportunities. Errors equate to opportunities for entrepreneurs who stay aware of and gain insight from other market participants and market conditions where product and service differentials bubble to the surface and can be realized. Spontaneously derived market knowledge guides entrepreneurial awareness.

Buyers, sellers, and investors have different information about economic conditions and differing views on what to expect in the economic long and short term. There is no such thing as perfect information about what customers want to support the production of products at any point in time. The entrepreneurs who are the most successful are flexible and resourceful, adapting and changing to market and economic shifts through innovation based on missed opportunities or inaction. It is also possible that, due to market errors and mistakes, firms and market participants may change to a direction that is the antithesis of their intended goals. Firms, managers, employees, customers, and investors all make decisions with asymmetrical knowledge.[61]

Market trial and error used by the entrepreneur do not derive from a static, evenly rotating economy. The question of whether buyers and sellers will effectively coordinate the use of such market errors to create new products or services alludes to the notion that not all people are entrepreneurial in their thoughts and actions. Therefore, since we do not live and operate under static economic conditions, it is presumable that errors, mistakes, or shifts in customer taste and preferences can be translated to opportunities, or provide a viable trade-off to do something new, or at least in demand. Likewise, in the best and worst market conditions, we can safely assume that the customer is looking at price, entrepreneurs are looking for supplies, investors are looking for capital, business owners are looking to serve customers, and individuals are looking for means to pursue their own ends via the market process. Everyone is searching for their next best option, even if that means creating or capturing market errors, malinvestments, or costly mistakes. Indeed, Rothbard said that entrepreneurial profit reflects the mistakes, errors, or malinvestments that were once apparent in markets that went unnoticed until the entrepreneur came along and jumped on the opportunity.[62]

There are many market participants—entrepreneurs, investors, customers. Entrepreneurs will attempt to achieve their aims and serve their customers with all the knowledge available to them. Entrepreneurs may find data or information from the spontaneous market or secondary sources. But the questions are always, "which source is indicative of the direction that market participants are

[61] Hayek, F. A. von. (1948). *Individualism and economic order*. Chicago, IL: University of Chicago Press.

[62] Rothbard, M. (2004). *Man, economy, and state*. Auburn, AL: Ludwig von Mises Institute.

trending?" and "What action does the entrepreneur intend to take to provide the psychological profit and prove beneficial to customer demand, despite the discrepancies in information obtained?"

Before the most recent technology boom in streaming and digitized products and services in the 21st Century, many firms thought technological products and streaming would be an overnight fad, but it was not. Entrepreneurs from many industries think that the newest technological products and services that are trending are worthwhile because adjusted and modified products close the error gaps that previous entrepreneurs overlocked. Examples of product errors and the trial by error adjusts include simple products such as the telephone, airplane, vehicles, cameras, and the computer and laptop, even dating platforms have modified the way in which people find friends and loved ones. These are iterations of products based on modifications through the change of data, and sometimes an entrepreneur's motivation of profit that perpetuates closing the gap on errors. Product errors and mistakes are neither good nor bad, but they are part of a complex process of many decision-makers trying to make their situation better in coordination with buyers' and sellers' plans. There is no way to ensure the rise of market conditions and the opportunity errors that might ensue. The best way to deal with any market condition is to maintain an entrepreneurial mindset. Another way to look at this, entrepreneurially speaking, is that the market can allow entrepreneurs to adjust conditions or errors by innovation. The spontaneous order of the market and its participants, participating and coordinating harmoniously, understand that making market errors is common. Do not be dismayed when errors occur—expect them!

Chapter 10: Entrepreneurs Miss Market Opportunities

"It often happens that sellers, who are too stubborn in keeping up their price in the market, miss the opportunity of selling their products or merchandise to their advantage and are thereby losers."[63]

Richard Cantillon, 1755

In his book *Capitalism, Socialism, and Democracy*, Schumpeter explained that introducing new production methods and new commodities to the market is inconceivable under conditions of perfect competition. Real-world competition, though, means some individuals capture an opportunity while others miss it. Some entrepreneurs have more knowledge about market conditions, and others have less. Some react and move quickly, while others react slowly. Businesses do not just fail—they miss entrepreneurial opportunities in the market and fail to *react* to consumer changes in time. Because Austrians conceive the market as a process and of competition as inspired by market participants, entrepreneurial innovation is the only way for a firm to survive. The notion of missed opportunities is rooted in Hayek's focus on knowledge and Israel Kirzner's idea of the interaction between the nature of the market and discovery. The fact is, one does not know what one does not know until they do know. Then, what does one do with the new knowledge?

In an era of constant change in consumer preferences—from conventional retail to omnichannel retail—many firms will undoubtedly miss entrepreneurial market opportunities because they are not learning from market signals. The question is: What did one learn, and when?

---

[63] Cantillon, R. (2010). *Essay on Economic Theory, An*. Ludwig von Mises Institute.

Many businesses do not just fizzle out. They do not learn from the Austrian view of markets, competition, and knowledge, and therefore miss market opportunities. Chains and established firms used old methods in a new competitive market and disregarded customers' metamorphosis from conventional to omnichannel—from customers who went from visiting a brick-and-mortar to accessing multiple channels (i.e., website, social media, phone) to purchase what they want. These businesses did not learn from experience how to improve their market position. They did not heed the market signals that the consumer gave them to cater to their newly emerging preferences. We are now living in a Schumpeterian era of innovation and quick-to-market activity that is the consequence of omnichannel consumerism. For entrepreneurs who are not on this innovation wave of providing goods and services when and how customers want them, it is an era of missed opportunities. Schumpeter noted, that the function of entrepreneurs is to reform or revolutionize the pattern of production by exploiting an invention or, more generally, an untried technological possibility for producing a new commodity or producing an old one in a new way, by opening up a new source of supply of materials or a new outlet for products, by reorganizing an industry and so on.[64]

Mises, Kirzner, and Schumpeter agreed that market adjustment according to customers' tastes and preferences. Not adjusting to consumer changes in tastes and preferences might account for why many firms close their doors and discontinue their services. What does this mean for existing market players during times of rapid market changes? The answer is that they must track market changes and adjust their business to the changes they observe. These changes present opportunities for the entrepreneur to stay in business and succeed.

Market distortions and economic interventionist policies created by the government can make these market opportunity signals foggy and unclear, which is why entrepreneurs must refine their ability to follow changes in consumer valuation. To improve entrepreneurial

---

[64] Schumpeter., p. 132.

perception and eliminate the fog, consider the following reasons why entrepreneurial leaders miss market opportunities:

- Entrepreneurs fail to see what customers want.
- Entrepreneurs do not co-create with their customers.
- Entrepreneurs do not foresee consumer transitions (e.g., from conventional to omnichannel).
- Entrepreneurs have not developed feedback loops between themselves and their customers (e.g., business-to-consumer or business-to-business).
- Entrepreneurs have not learned from previous experience new ways of bundling products and services in new market conditions.
- Entrepreneurs do not combine and recombine resources on time.
- Entrepreneurs cease searching for discoveries within and between new or existing markets.
- Entrepreneurs do not acknowledge that entrepreneurs and customers have incomplete and sometimes error-prone knowledge.
- Entrepreneurs are unsure about what works and neglect consumer-oriented just-in-time opportunities.
- Entrepreneurs miss relationships with customers; they do not ask questions, learn, and respond appropriately.

The timing to implement innovation is never clearly signaled. Entrepreneurs do not know the market's future, so they cannot act "just in time." Why? According to Kirzner, entrepreneurs make entrepreneurial errors as they pursue various ends, consequently changing other entrepreneurs' plans[65]. The change of plans and error is the very essence of opportunities that manifest themselves to the aware entrepreneur and it should be noted that only in a market economy can errors convert to an opportunity. Every market participant has error-prone knowledge and is subject to missed innovations and opportunities.

---

[65] Kirzner, I. M. (2015). Austrian Subjectivism & the Emergence of Entrepreneurship Theory. Indianapolis, ID: Liberty Fund.

How can entrepreneurs use knowledge, address market errors, and recognize market signals to pursue what lies ahead? Little bits of knowledge are scattered everywhere, making it possible for some entrepreneurs to get it right and adjust. Successful entrepreneurs judge the market correctly, as Kirzner wrote. However, numerous others judge the market incorrectly. They do not anticipate what is going on—they are subject to errors in judgment and the inability to see what is ahead, leading to missed entrepreneurial market opportunities. Knowledge is prone to error. That the market sends distorted signals to entrepreneurs (through no fault of their own) is not the result of market failure, but of market adjustments that result in missed opportunities. But note that the idea of missed market opportunities is not the same as opportunity costs. Missed market opportunities occur after learning something new, adjusting to consumer valuations, and applying the new knowledge. The omnichannel consumer is changing the market. Entrepreneurs—the disrupters/innovators—must alter their market approach. Those who lag behind market changes will miss market opportunities. Remember, the consumer is entrepreneurial, too!

In the Austrian sense of the term, entrepreneurs must find the innovative wave and jump in just in time to reap the benefits of market activity from missed market opportunities based on previous consumer interactions. Market-oriented entrepreneurs realize that they have a small window to adjust, employ innovations, capture conventional consumer valuation, and simultaneously reach the omnichannel consumer—just in time.

Chapter 11: The Entrepreneur and Human Capital

"The reason, I think, is that these young and relatively inexperienced executives knew three things as well as their own names. In other words, they understood our basic beliefs, and this understanding enabled them to move into unfamiliar jobs and to overcome the shortcomings they may have had in technical skills."[66]

Thomas J. Watson, Jr., 1963

Entrepreneurs do not fall out of the sky and they do not develop overnight—despite what some may think. Many variables must come together to produce an entrepreneur. One variable is human capital. When we think of the human capital that produces an entrepreneur, we tend to think of formal education. While this may impact success in many specialized fields, it is not that important in the pursuit of entrepreneurship. I think here of Henry Ford, Dale Carnegie, and John Merrick, the Black North Carolinian self-made banker. In each of these cases, there was more at work then what meets the eye, especially related to articulating knowledge and the unarticulated knowledge they employed in their entrepreneurial ventures that have changed the world.

Human capital *is* education, though—education composed of skills, values, talents, and variances of experiences from one's cultural background. An artist who picks up a paintbrush to create their first portrait might base future success on past results. However, others who have years of experience painting, and perhaps an associated formal education in that field, will have a head start on others who decide to use their formative years pursuing other endeavors. What matters with human capital is the accumulated experiences over time. Education is the long-term

---

[66] Watson Jr, T. J., (1963). A Business and its Beliefs: The Ideas that Helped Build IBM. New York, NY: McGraw-Hill.

accumulation of structured and or semi-structured personal reflection of scattered pieces of knowledge.

According to the Austrian school of economics, the effect of knowledge on entrepreneurial decision-making has an essential place in the economy. Knowledge in and of itself may serve a self-promoting purpose, but knowledge provides entrepreneurs with a sense of value in the market economy. As a form of human capital, knowledge ranges from knowing prices to knowing where best to allocate personal property, to knowing what to produce (or not) in any given market where customers have the final say.

How does knowledge become an applied skill for entrepreneurial pursuit? It happens through the application of production and/or discovery and alertness to market needs.[67] Skills are what people can do, maybe not much better than another person, but well enough to compete with another person with the same or similar skills. Most, if not all, entrepreneurs use their skillset as a launching point to start an enterprise. This may include skills gained from previous work experience, hobbies, and/or sheer happenstance. Life and educational experiences are paramount for one to become a specialist in the marketplace. Not to mention experiences and education assist in developing skills for identifying market errors, investing in errors, and brining opportunity errors to market.

What one had learned in their family and social circles is included in the skillset and knowledge-based development, as the fundamental transmission of values emerges from one's own family and social setting. Beliefs about human capital formed via family and social settings—whether positive or negative—are beliefs that either lead you to start your own business or discourage you from doing so. Social settings are the bedrock for skill and attitude development. The difference between entrepreneurs and everyone else is that entrepreneurs have used their circumstances to their advantage and advancement. Instead of using their skills to work for

---

[67] Kirzner, I. M. (1960). *The economic point of view: An essay in the history of economic thought.* Auburn, AL: Ludwig von Mises Institute.

an employer for reward, they chose to capitalize on their tangible and intangible human capital and work for themselves.

Many entrepreneurial studies fail to discuss the reality of trial and error and have failed to use missed opportunities for mediate and future human capital development. Adjusting error is mostly the same as learning on the job. Although you may initially lack experience while working with an employer, as you continue to spend more time on the job, you will learn the required skills. If the employee decides to pursue another employer, they can demand the market price for their newly developed skillsets. How is this scenario any different from, say, an upstart bicycle shop owner learning about the various bike styles across the globe, marketing new product lines, and learning QuickBooks for accounting to help establish their business?

Human capital's main idea is that individual skills based on market demand convert to market discovery. Therefore, in a more general sense, human capital is cultivated by others around the individual, the region in which the individual lives, and the values instilled in them early in their development. In other words, everyone in society reaps the benefits of the human capital that one obtains through the transmutation of transitioning raw materials to finished consumer goods. It is not to say that one cannot acquire skills late, but acquiring these skills later does not guarantee a future place in the market. Not having human capital skills is not deterministic but does have long-term effects on potential entrepreneurs' abilities.

What is deterministic and detrimental to potential entrepreneurs is the cultural or regional transmission of negative human capital. Not everyone seeks to be an entrepreneur or acquire human capital with market value, called negative human capital. However, negative human capital can often later be disregarded or overcome when circumstances change. Negative human capital can cause disdain of entrepreneurship. Cultures, and some whole nations, exhibit signs of negative human capital. Negative human capital is damaging to many early would-be entrepreneurs who are told by their peers, relatives, and others to live a way of life that does not provide the value, energy, confidence, or disposition to purse market opportunity.

Experiences, skills, and how to use them culminate in the period. Rome was not built overnight, and neither was the entrepreneur. No one was born with the required skills or credentials needed to be a practicing chiropractor. Education and experiences occurred over time, and a career came to fruition. The same holds for the entrepreneurial know-how that is called upon when a market opportunity is spotted. Circumstances must come together like the moon and sun align to create an eclipse.

The coming together of circumstances forms clusters of talent because of human capital. Some cultural and regional clusters in specific industries are more evident than others. The mainland Chinese migrated to Singapore, set up successful businesses, and overtook some Singaporeans' industries.[68] The phenomenon is even noticed between and among the same group of people. Some individuals choose to raise their human capital in a structured environment, while others prefer a lack of structure. There is no one best way to obtain human capital; it is accumulated over vast amounts of time to manifest itself at later dates. Therefore, it is the test of time and market conditions in which the individual will employ energy and be rewarded for their accumulated human capital to continue to act purposively as new conditions and institutional arrangement change over time.[69]

There is another factor of human capital expressed in the context of groups: ethnic characteristics and entrepreneurial networks.[70] Group clustering in urban areas creates a unique environment where human capital can be used and applied in the service and production industries. The favorable conditions leading to favorable market

---

[68] Clive.

[69] In the 1988 version of *Human Action*, von Mises defined presence of mind as the quickness with which individuals can adjust their thinking and action based on circumstances in which they act. He asserted that new conditions constantly arise, and therefore, an individual's adaptation is the acting man (p. 103).

[70] Light, I., & Bhachu, P. (1993). *Immigration and Entrepreneurship: Culture, capital, and ethnic networks*. New Brunswick, NJ: Transaction.

process in a market depends on the structure of the economic condition and where the reduction of economies of scale enables the opportunity to enter and effectively serve niche opportunities, maybe even using niche human capital.

Entrepreneurial migrating and emigrating groups gain and use similar human capital in various places over time. The twice migrant groups, i.e. cultural groups that have immigrated or emigrated between two or more countries aside from their native country, have migrated to different countries at different times with the same set of skills with little to no alteration.[71] These cultural groups assimilated to their circumstances because of economic conditions and acquired new human capital and entered new industries. There have been cultural groups that did not have a myth of return to their native country as they found entrepreneurial locations to employ their entrepreneurial skills. Examples of the myth of no return include cultural groups that have immigrated to and emigrated between: East Africa, the United Kingdom, the United States, and Canada. As these groups pursed entrepreneurial market niches in and between different countries, they learned new but relied on their conventional traditions, skills, and knowledge that date back to the time the group left their place of origin. The clockmakers, the peddlers, and the craftsman—adaptive groups the world over, and even the Chinese entrepreneurs in Southeast Asia—could utilize their unique human capital in the places to which they moved. And so can you!

---

[71] Bhachu, P. (1985). *Twice Migrants: East African Sikh settlers in Britain.* New York, NY: Tavistock. See pages 30-53.

Chapter 12: The Entrepreneur or The Engineer

"The engineer—as far as he attends to the technological side of his job—applies only numerical relations established by the methods of the experimental natural sciences; the businessman cannot avoid numerical terms which are the outcome of his understanding of future human conduct."[72]

Ludwig von Mises, 1949

The entrepreneur and the engineer do not take the same approach to a problem in a market economy. A market economy is full of unknowns about the movement, direction, and preferences of a consuming society. Both the entrepreneur and the engineer create wonders for our society. If it were not for the engineer, there would be no bridges, roads, or other structures constructed for our everyday use—the same is true of the entrepreneur. However, a further examination of the dichotomous way of thinking, i.e the entrepreneur or the engineer, about market discovery and discrepancy reflects a tendency to either view the market with fixes or adjustments that allow for errors to bubble up to the surface as potential market opportunities for entrepreneurially aware people to notice and grasps.

Too often, mistakes and errors are deemed unacceptable. People want to correct mistakes or control for a margin of error. While this thinking is necessary for the engineer, whose job is to ensure that a bridge does not collapse, to the entrepreneur, eliminating mistakes and removing errors is untenable if not self-defeating. Why? Because the very basis of entrepreneurial activity hinges on modifications and recombining resources for better products because of consumer demonstrated preferences, which can only come about because of a market mistake by other entrepreneurs and business owners. Eliminating the option of adjusting errors

[72] von Mises, L. (1951). *Profit and loss*. Auburn, AL: Ludwig von Mises Institute.

decreases the opportunities for discovery which takes away the role of the entrepreneur.

On the other hand, the engineer is trained to eliminate error for many reasons—including products, services that people use that require production processes and methods used to ensure usability and safety for human use or application. The engineer's error is specific, nuanced, and expert, and for the most part, can be controlled. The entrepreneur, though, does not seek to control the margin of error; the margin of error decreases by trial, which means putting forth many attempts to provide customers with what they want. The market conjoins with and assists in creating other industries that were either dormant or are altogether new. Engineers earn more when they construct safe and sound things for economical use; the same is true for entrepreneurs. Those who bring existing or new products to market, with subjectively valued quality and prices, are rewarded with the psychological benefit of profit. One profession (the engineer) eliminates errors and mistakes; the other (the entrepreneur) finds errors and mistakes that reward their awareness and swiftness to rework whatever it is to make anew. Therefore, profit is the index of undiscovered mistakes, and profit earned is a sign that an error existed.

The entrepreneur is not solely motivated by profit. Other motivating factors are clearly at work for both the entrepreneur and the engineer. However, the entrepreneur is a social being who seeks to make exchanges that leave both they and their customers better off than before. One may ask, how does each become better off because the entrepreneur is a social being? The engineer controls the environment in which many tasks occur; there are known objectives and (somewhat) known means of the employment toward those objectives. On the other hand, the entrepreneur has to choose scarce means to accomplish ends, albeit if their end is the consumption of their own economic productivity. Production begets production and relies on other people many of who one will never meet but serve at various times, places, and regions.

What makes the entrepreneurial action to adjust mistakes and errors through trial so vital is that the interaction between market participants should be spontaneous. No one person designed the market system. As each market participant becomes aware of what others want or are willing to exchange, a circular process ensues, and the process of creating markets and industries follows when investment from other entrepreneurs, which then develops a new standard that follows a boom in innovation.

In the early days of the American frontier, just before the Revolutionary War, peddlers would rush to the shore to buy imports they thought they could resell at a good enough price to win them some exchange value. Streets were rare. Peddlers walked or used wagons to reach villages to sell their wares. The carriage, furniture, and clock industries grew. Because of the American Revolution, clockmakers went into gunsmithing. Roads, maps, and thoroughfares developed at lightning speed across the country. With roads came tolls; with increased transportation, inns, hotels, and restaurants built along the main roads, where peddlers could grab food and sleep while traveling on business. These industries did not come into existence because of a plan, but because there were mistakes left to build upon and once they were corrected, it created whole new markets and industries much of which we enjoy today. Innovation has a snowball effect but does not happen overnight. Innovation is a struggle.[73] Nevertheless, the power of transition in the market shows how social interactions create environments where whole industries can be established.

The effect of social interaction is no different today with the advent of social platforms and cloud-based systems that allow entrepreneurs to reach people, suppliers, and investors and provide easy access to knowledge to make decisions. Many institutions that lead to successful inventions by entrepreneurs and capitalist in times past and present were not created—intentionally, but at various times and through unintended ways and reasons they were recombined to form those products that customers have come to

---

[73] Dolan, J. R. (1964). *The Yankee peddlers of early America.* New York, NY: CN Potter.

enjoy. The market process does not work well when there is engineering that attempts to prohibit, control, or suffocate social interaction where opportunities lay dormant.

What is meant by this engineering? If company A acquires an innovation from entrepreneur A, then company B, in the same industry as company A, has to acquire the same or better innovation to compete with company A. In the same way, company B has to change their business model and take a different market position due to company A gaining the newer technology that enables them to perhaps do more with less, thereby gaining more significant consumer share.

In the mid-1800's, iron was used by many companies as railroads proliferated throughout the United States. In the 1860's, the Bessemer Steel process made the open-hearth process obsolete, revolutionizing the iron industry. Mass retailers began to replace wholesalers, not by human design but through the natural process of adjustments. Positive obsolescence was due to the rapid speed of new technology, which resulted from the demand of the masses for cheaper and greater access to goods, and entrepreneurs discovering new ways to direct human effort and raw materials.[74] As can be seen from these examples, there are companies that because of innovation through trial and error acquired large market shares which was a long struggle to create. Entrepreneurs did not deliberately aim at a particular design, but it developed based on market demand at a point in time and through the passing of time. What is noticeable is how the market responded to the best use of resources as used between industries, and swiftness in response in the combination and recombination of resources adjusting to market signals much of which did not permit *fixing*.

Products can be engineered, but market activity cannot. If and only if the entrepreneur and customer socialize spontaneously in attempts to exchange goods that are of least value with each other will there be conjoining and development of new market industries.

---

[74] Chandler, A. D. (1977). *The visible hand: The managerial revolution in American business*. Cambridge, Mass: Harvard University Press.

Change and action are inevitable, and affect producer supply and consumer demand. You may ask if there is a difference between an entrepreneur and an engineer regarding their market economy approach.

The entrepreneur and the engineer have a diametrically opposed view of the best way to allow the market process to work. Views and actions affect decision making. "How do we fix" versus "what do I need to do less of" or "what happens if" are distinguishing statements. Why are the differences between the engineer and the entrepreneur matter? Because these differences are a direct reflection of decision-making in the long- and short-run and has significant implications for people's decisions in the market.

Everyone agrees that we need engineers to perform critical tasks for our society, but how an engineer approaches market changes and adjustments differs from how the entrepreneur approaches the same phenomenon. One deals with facts and figures and known predictive outcomes, while the other deals with the nature of things. Frequently, no facts or figures deal with the unpredictability of dynamic interactions between people in a society. Specific decision-making and engineering skills are requisites in building structures, aircraft, bridges, and technological devices. But the entrepreneur must make decisions on how to invest in these products and projects, determining the best use of resources, time, and production efforts, because of the dynamicism of change. The entrepreneur's requisite decision-making and visionary skills are suited for the market process's dynamic workings, discovery, innovation, and participant coordination.

Despite this realization, we have plenty of engineering-style commentators who seem to think it is best to employ engineering thinking to *fix* markets—they argue that if we put everything in place, fixing errors with deliberate aims, and the intended results will ensue. The entrepreneur understands trade-offs, errors-adjusting, perceptions, and incentives will shape the way people behave under various circumstances. For example, engineers can design software and iPhone, but there is no way to engineer the desire for consumers to buy them, or the most advantageous timeframe to cease the product production or produce a new style, control how customers wear them, or know if customers will choose to buy the shoes as collector's items rather than as something to wear. Engineers designed Facebook and many other platforms and software for consumption, but the usefulness will ultimately be determined by the consumer. People use social platforms for many things. Changes emerge after production, not before.

Fixing the economy does not include the principle of *trade-offs*. It is impossible in many ways to fix the economy or the conditions that are necessary for the entrepreneur to function. The difference in thinking between the entrepreneur and engineer rests on the assumption that if we fix A, then the effects of A will not persists, and if we fix B, then C will not cause effects, so put D over here, and E right here, and the total end result should ensue. Case in point, the entrepreneur has to think in terms of trade-offs and not in terms of fixing what is only controlled by market participants in the marketplace making decisions. The entrepreneur has a particular (subjective) vision for the market and how it is supposed to work or how it is to recover. Ostensibly, some objective is to fix the issue or problem as much as possible if something is wrong or seemingly amiss—meaning the economy is broken, so fix it. On the other hand, some understand that markets cannot simply be fixed. Markets can only be adjusted by using the institutions that exist, use of property, ingenuity, and cost-effective methods to serve customers based on what is wrong or missing in the market.

The next logical question is, how do you protect the importance of the entrepreneur? The quick answer is that we do not have a choice, because as long as customers change tastes or preferences, adjustments will be derived from errors in the market that are waiting for someone to apply their skills, ingenuity, and entrepreneurial vision. Moreover, the difference between thinking like an engineer and thinking like an entrepreneur concerns economic markets and market recovery. I expect an engineer to fix an airplane so that it is safe for flyers to travel, but I do not expect the engineer to use those same skills to fix an economy. That is why only market problems can be addressed and adjusted by entrepreneurial vision and ingenuity—without engineering fixes—which does not protect the entrepreneur. It is not a matter of fixing but a matter of asking: do we want more or less, and how, what, and who can do it best? *This* is what protects the entrepreneur.

Entrepreneurs rightfully understand that market problems can be tackled using their skills, energy, and resources. Producing and promoting products and services to those who want and need them is what entrepreneurs do best. When market problems are eliminated by simply "fixing" problems through noneconomic or noncompetitive measures, there is no longer work for the entrepreneur. Only when there is something wrong or adjustments needed in the economy is the entrepreneur protected. The entrepreneur's protection rests on the customer's moving subjective scale that determines product and service importance. The engineer does not require this kind of protection.

The market is the only place where when something is wrong, or a problem persists, it can be examined and adjusted to benefit everyone. This is done by those who have the resources and ability and those who do not (yet) have the skill but the energy and ingenuity to overcome barriers to market entry. Currently, we need entrepreneurs and small businesses to make needed adjustments in the market economy, which is not a matter of simple fixes, but of using individual vision to pursue the market opportunities in a coordinated effort. Now is the ideal time to protect entrepreneurs and small businesses and allow them to flourish in an unfettered market environment. Is this wishful thinking? Maybe. But now is the opportune time for anyone to find a market problem and try entrepreneurship. To serve in the economy, there is a strong need for one to create an entrepreneurial vision and not an engineering vision to eliminate errors and address them with fixes, which, when touted nowadays disregards the trial and error approach that the many who came before us implemented. Let the entrepreneurs find better and more productive ways to offer customers their goods and employ cost-effective methods of producing products. The economy does not need engineers but entrepreneurs.

Entrepreneurial profit is the index that shows that something needs to be discovered and adjusted in the marketplace.[75] There are, in other words, profit opportunities based on discrepancies between product prices and factors of product availability. What is the incentive for entrepreneurs to apply their vision and implement their resources to serving customers? Existing entrepreneurs and small business owners should be able to make market adjustments, alongside those willing to enter industries with their naivety who hope to make something better for you and me. We have gotten so far away from allowing naivety and genius to reveal new insights and the unskilled and skilled to innovate because society placed too much emphasis on experience in a particular endeavor. Many times, we hear of the results of the skilled or semiskilled entrepreneurs address solutions to customers' needs and market problems, but often those who were not experienced who made attempts at entrepreneurship go unheard of. There is nothing wrong with experience, but a market economy should be able to reward those who lack experience, so they are able to give society new insights.

Look at how long it took the contemporary stove to take over the fireplace's everyday use in the middle of the 19th century. If it were not for Benjamin Franklin's (Franklin) stove,[76] how would the fireplace transition to the stove? A host of examples provide evidence of the entrepreneurial vision to adjust market problems that were not human design but spontaneous order. Peddlers of the past had no road to connect with their customers, so they demanded that roads be built, which resulted in public transportation, which led to an explosion of inns and hotels.[77] Through these entrepreneurially minded individuals came rapid growth of cities with more customer demands. The demand for ice grew into a successful export for Frederic Tudor of Boston, coined the Ice King.[78] He and an owner

---

[75] Rothbard, M. (2004). Man, economy, and state. Auburn, AL: Ludwig von Mises Institute.

[76] Dolan, J. R. (1964). *The Yankee peddlers of early America.* New York, NY: CN Potter.

[77] Ibid.

[78] Ibid., p. 224.

of a pond revolutionized ice harvesting and invented the machine to keep ice frozen for long periods of time while in transport. It created an ice industry, even though they had no previous experience with ice!

We have similar opportunities today as the economy seeks to recover, but they can only be realized if the entrepreneur's role is protected, allowing them unhampered attempts to address limitless market problems and deliver options to us. The only people who change the rules of consumption are consumers. Who is best suited to do this? We do not need the precision of the engineer to address the "ever-changing reality, changes in value scales and resources of market participants"[79]—we need more entrepreneurship! By the nature of being human, we are prone to making honest mistakes. No one is perfect, our knowledge is incomplete, and no one is infallible, so we have to look elsewhere to identify perfection. It is a fact of life. These overlooked and unintentional market mistakes provide for up and coming entrepreneurially minded and motivated individuals to build upon mistakes others made before them. I think of the common call to stand on the shoulders of giants. Think about it: if it were not for mistakes made, there would be nothing to do better or upgrade to benefit future customers. There would be no use for underpriced and underutilized capital resources.

Mistakes and errors, for the most part, are seen by non-entrepreneurs as something to be eliminated. Products are created and produced imperfectly. Imperfections in products and inconsistency in services create the need for clashes of ideas in a market economy. Changes in customer preferences and underutilized or underpriced capital are significant signals to the entrepreneur seeking improvements. When it becomes apparent to the entrepreneur that resources have a better use than their current use, it entices the entrepreneur to grasp the opportunity. Without the entrepreneur, how will we know what resources are underutilized or scarce? The entrepreneur can only come to know this market

[79] Boorstin, D. J. (1965). *The Americans: The national experience.* New York, NY: Random House.

knowledge if the market is in perpetual motion—buying and selling the production factors and the correction of previously made mistakes.

Mistakes made unknowing to the entrepreneur, which may not manifest themselves immediately. Nevertheless, when the mistake becomes visible in the market, it becomes an opportunity for an entrepreneur.

Conclusion

Rome was not built in one day. Neither was the entrepreneur. Entrepreneurs are and always have been responsive to market conditions and changes. They are trend-setters and innovators. They are inspiring and enthusiastic and have served many regions around the world since time immemorial. Social, technological, political, and geographical changes are outside of the entrepreneur's control—but entrepreneurs, more than non-entrepreneurs, are more likely to adapt to changes and adaptations of an ever-changing market economy and economic institutions. F. A. Hayek explained the very essence of the development of the institutional framework under which the entrepreneur serves:

> "the successful combination of knowledge and aptitude is not selected by common deliberation, by people seeking a solution to their problems through joint effort; it is the product of individuals imitating those who have been more successful and from their being guided by signs or symbols, such as prices offered for their products or expressions of moral or aesthetic esteem for their having observed standards of conduct –in short, of their using the results of the experiences of others."[80]

Shane Scott explained how instrumental the right environment[81] is for the entrepreneurial spirit to emerge and flourish. The environment influences how entrepreneurs behave and to what extent they can operate to serve their fellow man. Whether entrepreneurs emerge from the technological or energy sectors, some rules and regulations work with or against them. Ever-shifting consumer preferences affect the demand for products and services. Fiscal and monetary conditions affect how entrepreneurs, investors, and consumers make financial decisions. Another benefit of a

---

[80] Hayek, F. A. (2020). The Constitution of Liberty. Chicago, IL: The University of Chicago Press.

[81] Scott, S. (2003). *A general theory of entrepreneurship*. Northampton, MA: Edward Elgar.

favorable market economy is that it brings forth visible adjustments, errors, new knowledge, and information to weigh entrepreneurs' subjective opportunity costs against the risk of pursuing an opportunity possibility. Entrepreneurs need to know if they are losing or making profit or losses—if there is a financial and psychological reward for the effort.

Throughout history, entrepreneurs have adapted to changing circumstances of all kinds. We have to agree with Scott: "When inflation is high or people do not expect economic or currency stability, they find it difficult to invest in entrepreneurial opportunities."[82] Subjective institutional arrangement considerations are essential for entrepreneurs as they decide what is best—to enter the market now or wait for more favorable conditions. People have moved around the globe to employ their entrepreneurial talents where they might best serve others; some individuals and groups have moved faster than others to find a favorable market, but eventually they all eventually found a community, region, or sector that rewarded the application of their resources, skills, and human capital.

Today, many of us do not have to move to sell a product or provide a service physically. Many can start and run a business anywhere; this is the current ubiquitous nature of business using technology. This does not mean there will be more entrepreneurs because there is an increase in business-related technology. Why? This is the million-dollar question. More technology equates to more entrepreneurship and the release of the creative spirit—one would think. But we must not forget that entrepreneurship is the work of a servant. Even the capitalist-entrepreneur seeks to serve others by investing in consumer goods or services and providing jobs, and in doing so, inspires others to seek an entrepreneurial opportunity one day.

Cantillon first coined the term *entrepreneur*. However, ancient records show novel commercial strategies of early merchants engaging in metalworks and textile exports during the times of

---

[82]Ibid., p. 149.

Babylon and Assyria.[83] Through the ages, the entrepreneur has adapted and transmuted many times over to reach the now novel status that is acclaimed today. In the 21st century, the novelty of entrepreneurship has changed; becoming an entrepreneur is a choice one can consider at any time not based on class or wealth. Historically speaking, the ideals of entrepreneurship have changed with the creation and reliance on technology and the realities of the market's many constraints. Paradoxically, however, the entrepreneur of today has more robust tools for the exploration of entrepreneurial opportunities. Never before in history has there been so much information at one's fingertips. Entrepreneurship is so deeply embedded in the human spirit—this spirit has the ability to serve others and oneself. Like Rome, the entrepreneur will face many challenges in the future. Rome has come and gone, but the entrepreneur is still with us. The entrepreneur is still a hero, always will be a hero to many of us and others in the future.

[83] Landes, D. S., Mokyr, J., & Baumol, W. J. (Eds.). (2012). *The invention of enterprise: entrepreneurship from ancient Mesopotamia to modern times.* Princeton, NJ: Princeton University Press.

No one's pupil

Made in United States
Orlando, FL
05 November 2026

90229823R10052